Chris Humphries

THE RESPONSIVE
CHURCH

ivp

THE RESPONSIVE CHURCH

LISTENING TO OUR WORLD

LISTENING TO GOD

Nick Spencer and Graham Tomlin

INTER-VARSITY PRESS
38 De Montfort Street, Leicester LE1 7GP, England
Email: ivp@ivp-editorial.co.uk
Website: www.ivpbooks.com

First published 2005

British Library Cataloguing in Publication Data
A catalogue record for this book is available from the British Library.

ISBN–10: 1–84474–099–4
ISBN–13: 978–1–84474–099–4

Set in Monotype Garamond 11/13pt
Typeset in Great Britain by Servis Filmsetting Ltd, Manchester
Printed and bound by Ashford Colour Press Ltd, Gosport, Hampshire

Inter-Varsity Press is the publishing division of the Universities and Colleges Christian Fellowship (formerly the Inter-Varsity Fellowship), a student movement linking Christian Unions in universities and colleges throughout Great Britain, and a member movement of the International Fellowship of Evangelical Students. For more information about local and national activities write to UCCF, 38 De Montfort Street, Leicester LE1 7GP, email us at email@uccf.org.uk, or visit the UCCF website at www.uccf.org.uk.

CONTENTS

ACKNOWLEDGMENTS

Although this book is a dual-author affair, a number of people stand behind it and we would like to take this opportunity to thank them personally for their support.

The two research projects that form the backbone of the odd-numbered chapters were only possible due to the vision and generosity of a number of people. *Beyond Belief?* was funded by Mike Elms who also commented perceptively and helpfully on the original draft of the analysis, as did Mark Greene and Brian Draper at LICC, and Revd Toby Hole.

Beyond the Fringe was the brainchild of Revd Yvonne Richmond, at the time a curate in the Coventry diocese. She successfully steered the project through from conception to completion, assembling a team of interviewers to conduct the research. Both she and her team – Rita Ashman, Colin Briffa, Margaret East, Bridget Harper, David Knight, Kate Mier, Keith Mobberley, Margaret Rose, Frank Seldon and Malcolm Tyler – and Sue Williams, who transcribed the interviews – deserve praise and thanks for their hard work and commitment. We are also grateful to Coventry Diocese's Forum for Parish Development and Evangelism, Springboard, Archbishops'

Council of The Church of England, St John's Church, Kenilworth, the London Institute for Contemporary Christianity, and the Group For Evangelisation (Churches Together in England) who, between them, funded *Beyond the Fringe*.

We have had a succession of helpful (and patient!) editors at IVP to whom we owe a debt of gratitude. Stephanie Heald originally proposed the idea for the book and passed the baton on to Sandra Byatt, who helped develop it before moving on to the more important business of giving birth to Anna and passing the baton on to Eleanor Trotter, who shaped the finished product and saw it through to completion, with encouragement, kindness – and patience.

We would also like to thank Alister McGrath for generously contributing a foreword.

This book is dedicated to colleagues at the London Institute for Contemporary Christianity, who have educated and encouraged Nick greatly over the last four years, and to the staff and students of Wycliffe Hall, Oxford, who have done the same for Graham for the past sixteen!

Nick Spencer and Graham Tomlin
Summer 2005

FOREWORD

Some years ago, a somewhat lightweight work entitled *The Myth of God Incarnate* made its appearance. The work made some interesting, though ultimately rather unpersuasive, criticisms of traditional Christian understandings of the identity and significance of Jesus Christ. Yet the most distinctive feature of this book was its core belief that the Enlightenment was something that was given and fixed for all time. It was *here*, and it was *right*. And that was that. For example, Professor Leslie Houlden argued that we have no option but to accept the rationalist outlook of the Enlightenment, and restructure our Christian thinking accordingly. 'We must accept our lot, bequeathed to us by the Enlightenment, and make the most of it.'[1]

That was back in 1977. Since then, things have changed dramatically. Throughout the Western world, the Christian church is faced with the challenges of adapting to cultural change. Public knowledge of the Bible is at its lowest for some considerable time, and many have little or no experience of Christian worship. Yet the assumption of the permanence of the Enlightenment world-view lingers on, particularly within those sections of the Christian community that, on the face of it, ought to be most critical of it. The rise of postmodernity has taken many older Christians by surprise, not least because the street credibility of older approaches to evangelism and apologetics has virtually evaporated. It is a profoundly uncomfortable situation for the church. How can it cope with postmodern culture, when so many of its chief apologists still live in a modern world?

Faced with this situation, Christians have reacted in a number of ways. Some are in denial about the massive cultural change we see around us, and struggle to maintain their churches as tiny outposts of orthodoxy in the midst of what they see as cultural madness. Others excoriate postmodernity as satanic, deluded or irrational, and work hard to get society and the churches back into the safe waters of the modern world-view. It is an understandable tactic. After all, Christians have become very experienced at proclaiming and defending the gospel within the Enlightenment world-view. Why not go back there?

Yet historians point out, not unreasonably, that contemporary Christians were appalled by the rise of precisely that modern world-view three centuries or so ago, seeing it as destructive of faith and as eroding critical Christian beliefs and values. Those concerns have long since been forgotten, but they need to be recalled. The simple yet awkward truth is that modernity and postmodernity are neither Christian nor anti-Christian, neither good nor evil. They are fundamentally cultural moods, each raising certain challenges and creating certain openings for Christian faith. Many Christians have got so used to working in a modernist culture that they have assumed that this was a permanent state of affairs – or, even worse, that it was somehow sanctioned by the gospel itself, despite the protests of their predecessors in the eighteenth century. As a result, they have been left bewildered by recent cultural changes, and have only two strategies at their disposal – trying to turn the clock back, or ignoring what is happening, and hoping it will go away.

This book is different. It offers a refreshing and intellectually compelling case for developing new ways of interacting with our culture. Nick Spencer and Graham Tomlin take John Stott's notion of 'double listening', and apply it with insight and enthusiasm to the many challenges we now face. This book is essential reading for those seeking to reconnect the church with our culture, and those within it who so badly need to hear the gospel – yet are prevented from doing so by the church itself. As a Reformation scholar, I have always been impressed by the early Protestant insistence that the gospel must be proclaimed and taught in a language 'understanded of the people' (Thomas Cranmer). If the gospel is proclaimed in a language that our culture cannot understand through a medium it cannot access, then the church has failed in its mission. It is just about as realistic as sending English evangelistic tracts to a people who, in the first place, speak French and, in the second, cannot read.

Spencer and Tomlin have done the church an immense service by showing how it can respond to change while remaining faithful to the gospel. Their culturally informed and theologically shrewd judgments will help the church regain its vision. This important and timely book will enable a new generation of Christian leaders to reach out into our culture. It deserves to be widely read, discussed and debated. I warmly commend it.

Alister McGrath
Professor of Historical Theology, Oxford University
Director, Oxford Centre for Evangelism and Apologetics

Notes to the Foreword

1. Leslie Houlden, in J. Hick (ed.), *The Myth of God Incarnate* (London: SCM Press, 1977), p. 125.

INTRODUCTION: THE PURSUIT OF HAPPINESS

Better off or just richer?

Do you own a radio? If the answer is 'yes' – and the chances are that it will be – you may be surprised to learn that you live in paradise and should 'cease to strive for further improvements'. If that sounds odd, it will be because you are reading this at the start of the twenty-first century rather than the end of the nineteenth.

In the 1880s, the journalist Edward Bellamy wrote a novel entitled *Looking Backward 2000–1887*. In it, a young man, Julian West, falls asleep and awakes on 11 September 2000. The America he discovers has left behind the industrial horrors of the nineteenth century and is now 'one great business syndicate . . . employing all citizens, who share equally in its profits.' During his tour of the future, West is introduced to a device that carries live music into people's houses by means of telephone cables. He is awestruck. 'It appears to me', he remarks, 'that if we could have devised an arrangement for providing everybody with music in their homes . . . we should have considered the limit of human felicity already attained, and ceased to strive for further improvements.'[1]

The wonder with which West describes the device we now call the radio appears, to us, charming. Bellamy, like many of his contemporaries, had complete faith in the capacity of wealth and technology to solve humanity's problems. Paradise was just a radio away.

Today, radios can be found in houses, cars, phones and hats. This most awesome of devices is now one of the most mundane, superseded by a series of entertainment and labour-saving products that would have been beyond Edward Bellamy's imagination.

The television is now ubiquitous – 99% of UK homes have one and the average household has around 2.5.[2] 89% have a video recorder, 83% a compact disk player, 54% a home computer, and 44% satellite, cable or digital TV. 99% of people have access to a telephone at home, 75% to a mobile phone and 44% to the Internet. 95% of homes have a refrigerator and a freezer, 87% a microwave oven, 54% a tumble drier, and 28% a dishwasher. Out on the drive, 73% of households have a car or van, 22% have two, and 5% have three or more. The majority of people in Britain live in a material paradise that would have left Edward Bellamy speechless.

Not only do we own more things but we also live longer to enjoy them. Life expectancy has risen by over 30 years since *Looking Backward* was published.[3] Infant mortality has fallen from 150 per 1,000 births to under 5. Medical progress and improvements in sanitation, hygiene, living conditions and nutrition have combined to contribute to a dramatic fall in the number of deaths by infectious disease. Tuberculosis, for example, which killed about 80,000 people in the UK in the year when *Looking Backwards* was published, killed 440 in 1997.

We travel further than ever before, holidaying more frequently and in more distant locations than our forebears.[4] We are better educated than at any time in the past. And, of course, we are wealthier. GDP per head, the economist's measure of our personal monetary wealth, has increased threefold since the Second World War and fivefold since 1900. We have more money than our grandparents would have known what to do with and we have much more to spend it on.

And yet, despite all this, we are no happier. Edward Bellamy's utopia did not appear. People did not 'cease to strive for further improvements' when they acquired radios. Nor when they bought their first TV, nor when they exchanged it for their first colour TV, nor when they bought their second, nor when they linked it to a video recorder, a DVD player and an X-Box. They did not stop striving when rising incomes, falling prices and domestic electrification enabled the purchase of labour-saving kitchen devices and removed the endless drudgery of physically exhausting housework. They were temporarily happier when they first acquired each new device but thereafter it made little difference. Paradise was postponed, at least until the next purchase.

Happiness (or life-satisfaction or well-being – various different terms are used interchangeably) is notoriously difficult to measure and one has to be careful before claiming with any confidence that a nation is more or less happy than it was in the past. Yet there are many indications that, in spite of the unprecedented economic growth and technological advances in the post-War period, we are actually *less* happy than we were fifty years ago.

One means of measuring happiness is by looking at its opposite: personal psychological ill-health.[5] According to the government's *General Health Questionnaire*, 29% of adults experience sleep problems, and about 10% experience depression, poor concentration, depressive ideas and anxiety. About 1 in 6 adults were assessed as having a neurotic disorder, 1 in 4 had a hazardous pattern of drinking, and 7% were alcohol dependent. Most of these levels had increased slightly since the time of the last survey in 1993.

In a similar way, another means of measuring society's satisfaction is to look at its opposite: crime. It's important to be careful when comparing long-term crime statistics, as ways of reporting, measuring and punishing crime change over time. Nevertheless, it is alarming that since 1950 the number of offences reported per 100,000 people has risen nearly tenfold and the number of violent offences twentyfold *despite* 50,000 more police officers and a threefold rise in the prison population.[6]

Perhaps the most reliable evidence is from what people themselves say about their happiness and life-satisfaction.[7] Such surveys have been conducted in many countries for around thirty years. In the most robust UK study, every year 2,000 people are asked this question: 'On the whole, are you very satisfied, fairly satisfied, not very satisfied, or not at all satisfied with the life you lead?'

In the early 1970s approximately a third of British people said they were 'very satisfied' with life. By the late 1990s that proportion was unchanged.[8] Referring to these findings, one academic paper notes laconically, 'life satisfaction has run approximately flat in Great Britain. In a period of increasing material prosperity . . . these results may surprise some observers.'

In reality, it is surprising fewer and fewer people, not least because it is a phenomenon seen across the Western world. Reported levels of happiness have been dropping for over thirty years in the United States. Despite a sixfold increase in income per head since 1950, the Japanese have recorded no increase in happiness.[9] In Belgium, the percentage of people who were very satisfied with their life fell from 44% in 1973 to 18% in 2001.[10] In the words of the economist Richard Layard, who delivered a series of lectures on economics and happiness at the London School of Economics in 2002:

> People in the West have got no happier in the last 50 years. They have become much richer, they work much less, they have longer holidays, they travel more, they live longer, and they are healthier. But they are no happier.[11]

This finding, that the dreams and aspirations of economists, politicians and utopians like Edward Bellamy have amounted to little, has understandably provoked much debate. Why, if we are physically and materially so much better off than our forebears, are we no happier?

Reasons to be cheerful

The obvious reason behind this trend, long preached by seers and sages, is that money does not make you happy. More and more studies are showing that beyond a certain point, income and happiness become decoupled.

More specifically, research has shown that happiness has less to do with absolute wealth than with relative wealth. Over a certain level that affords people life's necessities, the amount of money you earn and own has less influence on your happiness than the amount of money you have compared to your peers. People achieve a degree of their life satisfaction from comparison, and so when everyone is manically trying to maximize their income, everyone is effectively running to stand still. Envy, in other words, destroys happiness.

This problem is exacerbated by the very particular conditions of modern consumer societies. Having long ago secured for us what we need, consumerism is now oriented around fulfilling our wants and, beyond that, creating wants for products and services to fulfil. The history of mobile phones provides a good example of this.

Having been largely dormant for the first ten years, the UK mobile phone market exploded in the 1990s. It was powered, at first, by people buying their first mobile phone, and then by people upgrading to the next model, which was conspicuously smaller or better. Phones soon shrank to the smallest size feasible, however, and, at least until '3G' technology became available, technological improvements from one model to the next were too small to justify an entirely new purchase. New arguments for consumption were needed. This resulted in campaigns like the one that ran the advertising line 'Life has enough embarrassments without your mobile phone being one of them.' Unable to boast about size or new technological advances, the campaign chose instead to use social embarrassment and artificially provoked insecurity as a reason for purchase. In the cold light of analysis, such a tactic seems shallow, nasty and calculating, yet it is atypical only in its unsubtle transparency.

Once any society (such as ours) has shed its traditional social indicators, such as class, gender, religion, trade or region, and replaced them with brand identity, insecurity about your mobile phone's design can be a genuine concern – or, at least, it can be engineered to be so. If your identity and self-esteem are dependent on the things you own, your happiness is dangerously fragile. A marketing society preys on malleable identities and vulnerable self-esteem.

In a different way, our frantic chasing after economic growth has disrupted the personal and social relationships that are one of the surest guarantors of happiness. In their research paper 'Life satisfaction', Nick Donovan and David Halpern comment: 'A consistent theme of research into life satisfaction is that social relationships are very important. Having friends, supportive relatives, workmates are all correlated with satisfaction.'[12] Yet despite this, the constant demands to work harder, earn more, change jobs, and relocate invariably strain and sever exactly those relationships that we are supposed to be working for in the first place.

Nowhere is this more pronounced than in marriage. Donovan and Halpern write: 'Studies have consistently found that married people are happier than those who were never married, divorced, separated or widowed. This relationship holds across cultures and even when income and age are taken into account.'[13] And yet, as everyone knows, the number of marriages has gone into free fall since the 1970s, whilst the number of divorces has risen from 74,000 in 1971 to 148,000 in 2002.

Finally, serious and sober academic and government papers (sometimes reluctantly) acknowledge that religious adherence corresponds closely with happiness levels:

> Religious people report higher levels of life satisfaction. Research, mostly into Christianity, has found a correlation between life satisfaction measures and religious certainty, strength of one's relationship with the divine, prayer experiences and devotional and participatory aspects of religiosity. Both the effect of religious belief per se and the social benefits provided by participation in religious activities have independent effects upon life satisfaction.[14]

Even those commentators who disagree with this analysis of religion's *wholesale* beneficial impact agree that the intrinsic or personal aspects of religious belief (rather than the extrinsic or social aspects of adherence) have a positive effect:

> Research affirms that higher forms of spirituality . . . a search for meaning, for unity, for connectedness, for transcendence . . . contribute more to contentment than the rituals of church attendance and daily prayer – extrinsic manifestations of religion that may reflect nothing more than a desire for social acceptance, the internalisation of parental expectations, or an insurance policy against the possibility of an afterlife.[15]

Whichever explanation you prefer, the fact remains that serious, committed engagement with ultimate issues of spirituality, purpose and transcendence can improve your satisfaction with your life.

Hope for the church

All this *should* be good news for Christianity and the church. If people are beginning to recognize – and not just recognize but feel deeply – that there is more to life than chasing after wealth, they may start turning to a creed that has long preached this fact and that proposes an alternative way of living. If they begin to realize that envy breeds unhappiness, they may be open to a message that teaches people not to covet. If they become disaffected with the shallowness and fragility of hitching their identity to famous brands, they might search for a more consistent, reliable and meaningful personal identity.

If they begin to realize that they are unhappy because their pursuit of wealth is wrecking the relationships that make life worthwhile, they might be open to a faith that is fundamentally about relationships. If they yearn for community, they might be more likely to seek one out. If they are searching for meaning, thirsting for purpose, aching for transcendence, they might even turn straight to God.

All things told, a religious faith that is about relationships, community, purpose, transcendence and a secure personal identity, that embodies a culture that goes beyond money, that knows and lives the difference between value and price, that helps people to overcome their natural human tendency to look over their shoulder and to envy – that kind of religious faith could have much to gain in the twenty-first century.

It *could* have and there are some small, tentative signs that it does. As we shall see in later chapters, people are more 'spiritually engaged' today than they have been for many years. Over 10,000 adults, for example, are baptized each year. Some (non-religious) commentators have called for serious, counter-cultural, ecclesiastical engagement. The author of a document produced for a think tank called the New Economics Foundation wrote:

> Given the orthodoxy of the grow-earn-spend philosophy, the case for the church and other religious agencies to act as counter-cultures has never been stronger.[16]

Others reluctantly acknowledge that, like it or not, mankind is a biologically religious animal:

> The fundamental practical problem for atheists like Dawkins and me is that religious belief seems to be innate in man, part of our genetic make-up. There is an evolutionary explanation for this . . . people naturally have religious belief and will form religions. That being so, it is far better that

they belong to the great religions, which have accumulated a vast body of wisdom and experience over the centuries. If not, they will start new religions, and the slaughter house of the 20th century bears grim witness to the dangers of this. [17]

All this *could* be good news for Christianity and the church. But the brute fact is that, to date, it has not been, and there are no immediate prospects that this will change. This book explores why and what the church might do about it.

Quick to listen

The Responsive Church is an exercise in what John Stott has called 'double listening': listening to our culture, and listening to God. On the one hand, it seeks to listen carefully to what people outside the church really think about God, Christianity, Christians and the church itself. It draws on *Beyond Belief?*, a research project carried out in 2002–3 by the London Institute for Contemporary Christianity (LICC), in which forty non-church-attending agnostics were interviewed about a range of issues, from their understanding of the Christian faith to their opinions on life in Britain today.

Following this, LICC engaged in a second research project in partnership with the Diocese of Coventry. This study, *Beyond the Fringe*, was the brainchild of Yvonne Richmond, then a curate in the Coventry diocese, who assembled a team of interviewers to conduct one-to-one discussions with sixty agnostics and atheists, in an attempt to understand their spirituality in the broadest sense of the word.[18] These two in-depth, 'qualitative' surveys are placed in the context of a number of 'quantitative' or statistical research studies that have been conducted in the UK over recent years, exploring the broader nature of religious and spiritual beliefs.

The point of this exercise is not to make the church market-driven, to rebrand the gospel as a consumer product or because we believe the *vox populi* is the *vox Dei* – far from it. This book tries to be careful, thoughtful and, above all, critical as it listens to these voices. Sometimes what they say needs to be politely ignored. At times the criticism is misplaced, misleading or simply wrong, and to follow it would be to strip Christianity of its very identity.

However, the fact that some of what the people had to say was mistaken does not mean we should dismiss it altogether. People have reasons, sometimes understandable reasons, for why they do not believe in Christ or go to church. Sometimes we can learn as much or more from our critics as we can from our friends. At the very least, the church needs to listen to its critics, to see whether they do in fact say some things it needs to hear. They may put their finger on some key issues for the church today which are easier to see from the outside than the inside, and which will help the church rediscover more of its calling and purpose.

Sometimes Christians think they know what people 'out there' think, but often such surmises are more anecdotal than actual. Are the unchurched hostile, ill informed or simply disengaged? Is it God, Christianity, Christians or the church that puts them off? Conversely, is it people's own lives – their beliefs, opinions, attitudes and habits – that deter them from embracing, exploring or even considering Christianity? The research presented in this book aimed to find out.

As it listens to these voices, this book is striving for a sympathetic, close and critical listening to what people really say and think about the church. At the same time, it attempts to listen carefully for God's word for the church in the light of what others are saying about it, by going first to the Bible and to Christian theology for wisdom. It will try, on the one hand, to weigh what these voices say in the light of Scripture and, on the other, to listen for what God is saying to us in this situation through the pages of the Bible. It takes the view that Scripture is the touchstone by which we should measure all things and the light by which we need to walk. Sometimes listening to these critics of the church helps us see things in Scripture we have not noticed before. If these voices from outside tell us where we are, we can expect Scripture to point the way we need to go from here.

The book is divided into four sections, each looking at a different area – God, Christianity, Christians and church – and highlights different features that UK churches need to think carefully about if they are to respond wisely to their critics: spirituality, apologetics, public image and communication. The order doesn't suggest a hierarchy of importance for these, but simply follows the order of what people think about God and the spiritual realm in general (Section 1), about Christianity specifically (Section 2), about the people who embody it (Section 3), and about the community or institution that they form (Section 4). Each section consists of a chapter (written by Nick Spencer) presenting the results of the two research projects mentioned above, and a second chapter (by Graham Tomlin) that weighs and considers these findings in the light of Christian theology. In doing this, the second chapter in each section begins to sketch out how the church might appropriately and sensibly respond to what people think of it.

Our hope is that this exercise will enable churches and their leaders to be more attuned both to the God who still speaks to his church, and to those people whom God loves, yet who do not find church attractive, credible or satisfying. Perhaps by listening to both, the church can help bring the two together.

Nick Spencer & Graham Tomlin
April 2005

Notes to the Introduction

1. Edward Bellamy, *Looking Backward 2000–1887* (Ticknor, 1888).
2. This figure, and subsequent ones, come from *Living in Britain: The 2002 General Household Survey* published by the Office for National Statistics (www.statistics.gov.uk). The figure of 2.5 TVs per household is from www.ofcom.org.uk.
3. See J. Hicks and G. Allen, *A Century of Change: Trends in UK Statistics since 1900* (House of Commons Research Paper 99/111).
4. See Office for National Statistics, *Transport Trends 2003*.
5. See Office for National Statistics, *General Health Questionnaire*.
6. J. Simmons and T. Dodd (eds.), *Crime in England and Wales 2002/3* (Home Office Statistical Bulletin, July 2003), Table 3.05; Hicks and Allen, *A Century of Change*, op. cit., Sections V and VI.
7. Such surveys have obvious problems (e.g. being susceptible to moods and circumstances), but are conducted and analysed in ways that address these issues. See Richard Layard, *Happiness: Lessons from the New Science* (Allen Lane, 2005), and Clive Hamilton, *Growth Fetish* (Pluto Books, 2003).
8. Andrew Oswald and David Blanchflower, 'Well-being over time in Britain and the USA', *Journal of Public Economics*, 2004.
9. Richard Layard, 'Happiness: has social science a clue?' (London School of Economics, Lionel Robbins Memorial Lectures, 2002/3).
10. Nick Donovan and David Halpern, 'Life satisfaction: the state of knowledge and implications for government' (Prime Minister's Strategy Unit, 2002).
11. Layard, 'Happiness', op. cit.
12. Donovan and Halpern, 'Life satisfaction', op. cit.
13. Ibid.
14. Ibid.
15. Hamilton, *Growth Fetish*, op. cit.
16. Richard Reeves, *The Politics of Happiness* (New Economics Foundation, 2003).
17. Andrew Kenny, 'Down with superstition', *Spectator*, March 2004.
18. The analysis of both research projects is available via www.licc.org.uk.

SECTION 1 | **GOD**

People in Britain today tend to believe in God, but in a rather colourless, theoretical and, above all, impersonal God. Whilst being credible, this deity is uninspiring, with little relevance to everyday life. Perhaps because this God is so unsatisfying, more and more people are exploring other spiritual avenues in search of meaning and purpose. These trends point towards our innate human desire for intimacy with God and with other people, and call the church to respond to this changing spiritual landscape by providing opportunities for authentic encounter with God and others.

1. SACRED HUNGER

A stubborn God

Secularism's big hope was that the advance of scientific knowledge would one day banish religion to the history books. Christianity and other faiths, so it was argued, were little more than primitive scientific theories that, once disproved, would fade from memory. Education would liberate people from the strictures of ecclesiastical dogma and leave them everywhere echoing the words of the French mathematician and scientist Pierre-Simon Laplace who, when asked why he did not mention God in his book on celestial physics, replied, 'I have no need of that hypothesis.'

More and more social research is proving this theory wrong. Europe is the most secular continent on earth and the UK is one of its most secular countries, yet research even in the UK continually shows that the vast majority of people believe in God.

Because it is very hard to ask people directly whether they believe in God (they usually respond, 'It depends what you mean by "believe" and by "God"'), when the annual British Social Attitudes survey examined theistic belief in 1998, they offered people a choice of six different statements and asked them to indicate which came closest to their position.[1]

The results showed that 21% of people agreed with the convinced theistic statement 'I know God really exists and I have no
doubt about it'; 23% agreed with the slightly less confident one
'While I have doubts, I feel that I do believe in God'; 14% of respondents agreed with the more hesitant statement 'I find myself
believing in God some of the time, but not at others'; a further 14%
agreed with the vaguely theistic sentiment 'I don't believe in a personal God, but I do believe in a Higher Power of some kind'; only
15% agreed with the openly agnostic statement 'I don't know
whether there is a God and I don't believe there is any way to find
out'; and only 10% agreed with the openly atheistic one 'I don't
believe in God' (3% did not answer the question). By this reckoning,
72% of people in late-twentieth-century Britain were theists of
some kind, compared with 15% who were agnostics and 10% who
were atheists.

More recent surveys have broadly corroborated these findings. An
ICM poll conducted for the BBC programme 'What the world thinks
of God', broadcast in early 2004, reported that 46% of people in
Britain say they have 'always believed in God', 10% that they 'believe
in God, but have not always done so', and 11% that they 'do not
believe in God but . . . in a higher power'. In comparison, 10% said
that they have 'never believed in God' and 6% that they 'used to
believe in God but no longer do so'.[2]

A third survey, conducted for the *Sunday Telegraph* in 1999,
reported that 71% of people believe in God, and three other surveys
from recent years recorded 60%, 62% and 64% of people saying they
believed in God.[3] A century of secularization does not seem to have
had much of an impact on levels of theistic belief in Britain.[4]

And yet, there can be little disagreement that Britain is one of the
most secular nations on earth, with levels of public and private religiosity, such as church-going, prayer and Bible reading being far
lower than in most other countries. Squaring this circle of stubbornly high levels of belief in God within a profoundly secular
culture seems difficult at first, until you explore the *kind* of God that
people believe in. That God may be surprisingly persistent in his
presence but, for many, his presence might just as well be an
absence.

Two kinds of God

The two samples of people interviewed for this book were deliberately recruited so as to exclude convinced believers in God. Nevertheless, while the number of agnostics was artificially inflated, there were still comparatively few outright atheists, reflecting the generally low proportion of people who are willing to dismiss the idea of God altogether.

Those who did completely reject God tended to do so for Laplace-like reasons. They saw God as 'a supernatural entity which people created, to cover all the answers to the questions they didn't know'. God was a primitive scientific theory, whose continued existence in modern society was no longer tenable.

Those atheists who did not reject God for this reason, rejected him because he was little more than a cartoon caricature. The image they had of God was clearly absurd, and for some this was the final word on the subject. Others were more tentative in their rejection but rejected him all the same. As one young woman said, 'I can't relate to a man with a big beard sitting on a cloud somewhere. That does not feel real to me.'

At the other end of the scale, some people (none of whom, it should be remembered, were church-goers) dismissed atheism altogether, expressing a certainty that one would more naturally expect to hear from convinced believers. Atheists, one respondent suggested, were spiritually stunted people, '[neither] spiritually [nor] intellectually very mature . . . [and not] spiritually-minded enough to grasp things that are highly academic in some ways'.

More common than either of these positions was the hesitant and vague belief in which God's possible existence was acknowledged, whilst being rephrased in less overtly traditional language (e.g. 'supreme power' instead of 'God') and hedged about with caveats (e.g. 'I don't know'), as with this elderly woman's evident uncertainty:

> Well, I suppose you could go to science and dismiss God altogether, but I think there is some sort of supreme power that is shaping our world, but what, I don't know.

This vague God had, not surprisingly, a rather vague nature, and what gradually emerged was a curiously divided being, who existed in two somewhat disconnected forms: God-the-theory and God-the-person.

God-the-theory was often described with the word 'he' but was, in reality, more of an 'it'. His characteristics were predominantly abstract, with words like 'energy' or 'force' being widely used to describe him. People said things like, 'I would imagine him to be energy' or '[he is] a spiritual force, an energy that runs and flows between all of us', or called him 'the great spirit' or the 'manifestation of all things good'.

His job was to create the universe and perhaps to oversee that creation in some unspecified way. He existed as 'a free roaming spirit . . . everywhere and in everything' or 'within me' or perhaps in a different dimension altogether, as one interviewee suggested:

> I read something years and years ago . . . called the 'flat earth' theory. What you have to imagine is that the world is actually flat and only exists in two dimensions, so you have all these flat people and everything is flat. But there is a third dimension which we know about but the flat earthies won't be able to understand . . . because they only know about two dimensions. Therefore if there is a fourth dimension that we don't know about, maybe that is where God is – I don't know.

This theoretical, abstract God was credible. He was, not, however, especially interesting or relevant to people's lives. He was neither personal in his nature nor intimate in his interests. As one of the most sceptical interviewees explained, he could not realistically be expected to be interested in human beings:

> If there is some sort of – I don't like to use the word 'supernatural' – some sort of being on whom the existence of the universe depends, then that being by definition would have to be so vast and complex that even beginning to understand would be far beyond any human, given the scale and perplexity of the universe. I find it extremely difficult to believe [that] such an entity . . . would have such a detailed interest in individual beings as insignificant as we are.

In as far as he existed, he was something like a mathematical theorem – an elegant proof capable of answering certain abstract questions but unrelated to the things in life that actually mattered to people. He was the God of whom people essentially thought, 'Yeah, God exists, but so what? It's of no importance to me.'[5]

God-the-person was, in contrast to this, relevant but rather less credible. He was meaningful and even important but far too much like a fairy story or the traditional caricature of God to be believable. This absence of a plausible image for who God-the-person might be either drove people to atheism, as noted above, or, as here, inclined them to God-the-theory:

> I say 'It' rather than 'He' or 'She'. In many respects that is where I start sailing close to the wind, because I don't see a God as sitting on a cloud struggling with a harp and all that. I see it [as] a much more tangible theory [or] concept.

Irrespective of God-the-person's implausibility, he was at least interested in human beings. Being involved with humanity almost came with his territory, a sentiment that pointed towards a hunger for a meaningful, intimate relationship with him that God-the-theory could not provide.

The problem was, of course, that whilst God-the-person was more meaningful than God-the-theory, he was rather less likely to exist. This was not necessarily an insuperable problem, however, with the *desire* for a personal God often being enough for respondents to engage with him, albeit casually and tentatively.

For some people, this relationship was based on wish fulfilment with a caricature God, but that did not necessarily mean that it was unhealthy or that it should be discouraged. One elderly man said, 'I don't think there is a God up there,' but he thought that 'all good believers have got God in their mind and think of him as an old man with a beard'. 'When they are in trouble,' he continued, 'they think about him and . . . try to get inspiration from him.' 'God can't do anything for you,' he explained, 'but he can help you do something for yourself.' For him, at least, the strength some people could draw from this enervated, slightly cartoonish God was enough. 'Let's keep the thought of him alive. Don't ever say or even think anything about people that think they rely on the presence of God – that is their prerogative. That is their prop.'

For others, God was more probable, a 'definite maybe' who was treated tentatively but seriously. He might offer guidance, comfort and possibly even judgment. Alternatively, he might simply be there, 'someone you call upon if you are in distress or when you haven't got anyone else to talk to'. Accordingly, people prayed to him, although prayer itself was a rather 'religious' term and was often avoided for that reason. Instead, they might simply talk to him, as one widowed interviewee said she did:

> If I have got problems I go to the big man upstairs . . . I talk to him. I don't pray, I just talk. I talk to him most of the time . . . I usually say good morning to him and goodnight to him when I go to bed. He is just there.

Such prayer need not have a particular point to it. One middle-aged mother explained that 'providing you are willing to accept his answer and it might not necessarily be the one you want, then, yes, there is a communication there'.

This positive attitude towards communicating with God was surprisingly widespread. Such an approach to 'prayer' might seem strange but it is, in reality, a wholly logical response to the inner voice that compels you to believe in God, convinces you that the only God worth believing in is one who is interested in your affairs, but reminds you that that God-as-person is neither credible nor intellectually defensible. The result is prayer that is protected by a shoulder-shrugging 'it can't do any harm; there may be a psychological benefit' attitude – an attitude articulated time and again by the people we interviewed. It was prayer for which 'it doesn't really matter whether there is or isn't [an answer], because it is still comforting to have that feeling'. It was prayer that 'you are not going to get any answers from . . . but [that will enable you] to get all your worries off your back [and] relieve the stress'. It was prayer that did not even need words. 'How I relate to the great being . . . is by being still,' one interviewee said. It makes a difference 'because I think I am doing something positive'. After it, 'you feel that you have done something and it makes you feel better in yourself'.

It should be noted that for a sizeable minority of the people who were interviewed, the psychological benefits of prayer were insufficient. They were less than impressed by the lack of an answer from prayer and unwilling to smile on the activity for its positive emotional effect. For them, what they saw as a one-way conversation was not enough. It felt as if 'you are speaking to yourself most of the time', and prayer did 'nothing [to] make me feel that I am having a two-way conversation'. For them, it simply meant that God-the-person was not there.

In spite of these frustrations and disappointments and the fact that God-the-person was nothing like as credible or probable as God-the-theory, there was a surprising amount of relating to him going on among the people interviewed. Relationships might have been irregular, tentative, skeletal and conducted *in spite of* what people believed rather than because of it, but they were still real. The human desire for meaningful contact with God overrode the apparent absurdity of the relationship.

That said, the incredibility of God-the-person effectively privatized that relationship. Few people spoke confidently about their communication with God-the-person for fear of appearing naïve or being asked to justify their behaviour, and that left only the cold and rather bloodless God-the-theory open to discussion. This privatization of relationship also left a vacuum for other, more socially acceptable, spiritual beliefs to colonize.

Innate spirituality

If belief in and prayer to God has stubbornly survived decades of insistent secularization, other, less orthodox, spiritual beliefs have positively flourished. Comparable surveys in 1987 and 2000 measured the percentage of people reporting some kind of spiritual experience (using the term broadly) over the previous twelve months and showed an increase in every category.[6]

The proportion of people detecting 'a patterning of events' rose from 29% to 55%. The percentage detecting 'an awareness of the presence of God' increased from 27% to 38%. Those sensing an 'awareness of prayer being answered' moved from 25% to 37%; those feeling an 'awareness of a sacred presence in nature' from 16% to 29%; those perceiving an 'awareness of the presence of the dead' from 18% to 25%; and those noticing an 'awareness of an evil presence' from 12% to 25%.

Perhaps most importantly, these increases were not powered by a small selection of superspiritual mystics, who claimed to perceive everything whilst leaving the rest of the population unmoved. The overall percentage of people who claimed to have experienced *any* of these events rose from 48% to 76%. Less than a quarter of the people interviewed felt nothing.

This rapid rise in what might be called 'spiritual awareness' is supported by other research. According to the market research company MORI, 24% of people claim to believe in faith healers, 28% in psychics and mediums, 31% in astrology, 32% in out-of-body experiences, 38% in ghosts, 40% in guardian angels, 42% in telepathy, 54% in premonitions or ESP, 57% in déjà vu and 60% in near-death experiences.

Perhaps even more surprisingly, the same survey reported that 8% of people claimed that they had had an out-of-body experience, whilst 8% said they had had 'personal experience' of faith healers, 12% of a near-death experience, 13% of psychics or mediums, 17% of telepathy, 17% of guardian angels, 19% of ghosts, 26% of premonitions or ESP, and 47% déjà vu.[7]

Other surveys show similar results for belief in and experience of such supernatural and paranormal phenomena. Whatever one makes of these figures, they do not paint a picture of a coldly rational, stubbornly logical, secular people. Once again, the picture of an ever-secularizing nation that was confidently drawn in the 1960s fails to convince. The public realm, never itself blatantly religious, may have been secularized, but spirituality, just like types of theistic belief, has, in response, 'gone underground'.

This rise in spiritual belief reflects the fact that human nature abhors a spiritual vacuum, and the privatization of God-the-person has created such a vacuum. If the tenets of 'official' religion no longer fill the gap (something we shall explore in Chapter 3), other beliefs will flood in. This was expressed well when MORI analysed some of the big social trends that have shaped Britain since the Second World War:

> What has certainly changed [since 1950] is that there is more acceptance of 'new age' spiritualism, and other supernatural phenomena . . . [In] a 1999 MORI Social Values question . . . 65% of the public agreed that 'Personal

spiritual experience is more important to me than belonging to a church.' This leads to what some would describe as a more credulous society. In January 1950, only 10% of the public told Gallup they believed in ghosts, and just 2% thought they had seen one. By 1998 we found that 40% now say they believe in ghosts, and 15% that they have 'personal experience' of ghosts; 6%, indeed, said they had based a decision on their belief in ghosts. Similarly, in 1951 only 7% of the public said they believed in foretelling the future by cards, and 6% by stars; in 1998, 18% of the public said they believed in fortune telling or tarot, and 38% in astrology.[8]

As the philosopher John Gray has written, 'religion has been repressed from consciousness in the way that sexuality was repressed in Victorian times . . . The result is not that the need disappears, but rather that it returns in bizarre and perverse forms.'[9] Religiosity and spirituality may have been suppressed in the public sphere, but surveys show that they survive powerfully, if vaguely and tentatively, in the personal.

The people interviewed for this book spoke openly and often willingly about a range of supernatural and paranormal topics, which divided into two broad categories: those that people deemed to be inherently less credible and meaningful and those that people thought were more believable and interesting. The first group, which included magic, trances, déjà vu, horoscopes, premonitions, visions and out-of-body experiences were often peremptorily dismissed, unless the interviewee or a close and reliable friend or relative had experienced it themselves.[10] The second group was equally disparate and included ghosts, miracles, angels, meditation and prayer. Ghosts were widely perceived to be souls that had not yet found rest and were often described in pseudo-scientific terms. They were people who had 'died . . . [with] unfinished work', or were 'energy passed into spirit', or were 'discarnate entities that . . . haven't gone on to the place where they need to be'.

Angels were thought to be people who had died and were now looking over you. They were sometimes thought to be conspicuously good people, sometimes close relatives and sometimes just people in general. Rather like God-the-person, even if they didn't actually exist, they were still useful and inspiring. As one middle-aged man said, 'I don't think there are any, but they fill a very good spot in our minds and vocabulary . . . [a] good word and influence.' Prayer, as noted, was often essentially a form of meditative communication, indulged in sporadically and for primarily psychological reasons. It offered you strength and comfort, even if it was a rationally indefensible activity.

A further indication of people's spiritual hunger could be seen in their engagement with the big questions of life. Significant as their attitude to angels, ghosts and prayer is, it is important to recognize that this is a very narrow and rather misleading definition of spirituality. Treating 'spirituality' as simply a question of the paranormal is to trap it in an esoteric niche that fails to reflect the breadth of the term. Properly speaking, spirituality extends beyond the supernatural to include questions of ultimate meaning. As one young man said:

> You like to think there is something after death. I mean, what have you lived, say, 50 or 60 years for? To die? You could say that everyone is spiritual because everyone thinks about that at some point.

This viewpoint was reflected in the fact that, when asked the question 'If there was one question you could have answered, what would it be?', *every* interviewee responded positively. Every individual – no matter how sceptical, atheistic, secularist or materialist they claimed to be – had 'big', metaphysical questions they wanted answering. Even those who insisted that human beings are 'merely' animals, without soul or eternal destiny and fated to rot in the grave, had big questions to which they wanted answers.

These questions divided broadly into five areas. The most important were about destiny. 'What happens after we die?' or 'Is there life after death?' or 'Is there an afterlife?' were the most frequently asked and keenly considered questions.

Secondly, there were questions of purpose, such as 'What is the meaning of life?' or 'Why are we here?' As one student remarked, to ask that question is almost the definitive characteristic of what it is to be human:

> People have always got that thing in the back of their heads as to 'Why we are here?' There must be a reason. I don't care whether people say

they don't believe in God or whatever. They have still got that thought in the back of their head. It is instinctive in everyone.

Thirdly, there were questions about creation, usually about the origins, size and meaning of the universe, such as 'How did it all start?' and 'Where does it end?'

Fourthly, and often linked to the first three issues, were questions about God and the spiritual realm. These were occasionally about God-the-theory but more often about God-the-person and his relevance to my life. People asked, 'What is it – this spiritual essence that I have been searching for and trying to understand?' or 'Am I here to serve a particular purpose?' – linking such questions to God in such a way as further to underline the need for God to be personally interested in who I am rather than just being intellectually credible.

Finally, there was the question of suffering, often phrased in abstract, philosophical terms but, as we shall see in Chapter 3, engaged in in resolutely personal ones.

These five questions were answered in a wide variety of ways, the answers revealing a great deal about respondents.[11] Their significance for our purposes lies in their ubiquity and importance. God's stubborn if rather divided and privatized survival, the growing awareness of the sacred in so many areas of life, and the emergence of widespread, 'new age' spiritual beliefs all find an echo in the persistent, all-pervading questions of life that people ask. To be human is to ask questions of purpose and destiny, almost irrespective of how publicly or intellectually acceptable those questions are.

The task facing the church is to respond to this spiritual hunger, whilst remaining true to the gospel message. It is to answer the charge laid by one critical interviewee, that 'the church could be tried in a court of justice and found guilty of killing off spirituality', without simply jumping on an increasingly crowded spiritual bandwagon.

Notes to Chapter 1

1. See Office for National Statistics, *Social Trends 1998*.
2. See 'What the world thinks of God' on www.bbc.co.uk.
3. MORI/*Sunday Telegraph*; MORI/*The Heaven and Earth Show*; ORB/*Soul of Britain*; MORI/*Sun*.

4. For some possible reasons for this, see Alister McGrath, *The Twilight of Atheism: The Rise and Fall of Disbelief in the Modern World* (Rider, 2004).

5. Quoted in 'Let the people speak', Church Survey Report (Ecumenical Research Committee, 2005).

6. ORB/*Soul of Britain*, 2000.

7. MORI/*The Heaven and Earth Show*, 2003.

8. MORI, *British Public Opinion 2003*.

9. John Gray, 'The myth of secularism', *New Statesman*, December 2002.

10. It is worth noting that these responses did not reflect the generally higher levels of belief in the paranormal that quantitative surveys report. Paranormal beliefs and experiences are hard to defend and, while people often have a sense that there is something paranormal 'out there', they are often reluctant to admit so in a situation, like a one-to-one interview, where they may be required to explain or defend it. As a result, quantitative surveys (which do not demand further justification) often report higher levels of belief than qualitative ones.

11. See Nick Spencer, *Beyond the Fringe: Researching a Spiritual Age* (Cliff College, 2005).

2. INTIMATE SPIRITUALITY

In the seventeenth century, an intense and quite brilliant young French philosopher had the idea of putting together a proper defence of Christianity. His aim was to commend it to the people he knew only too well – the kind of cultured despisers of religion who had no time for it. In explaining why people do turn to believe in Christ, he coined one of the best-known phrases in Western literature: 'The heart has its reasons, which reason cannot understand.'

The young man was Blaise Pascal, and he had noticed something very important – that, despite what increasing numbers of people were saying in his own time (including his great contemporary, René Descartes), everything doesn't get decided by purely rational processes. Pascal's point was that we choose certain things and not others, not because we always think it out rationally and come to logical conclusions, but for reasons that often we don't know about ourselves. We are not just minds on sticks. We are complex mixtures of heart, mind, will and feeling.

His argument was ahead of its time. The seventeenth century saw the origins of the Enlightenment, the 'Age of Reason', where every idea was tested at the bar of reason, and if it could not be proved, was relegated to irrelevance. This was a confident age, sure of itself, sure in particular that it knew what counted as true and false, and how to tell the difference – by applying rational thought processes to it. Notions that claimed to be true but were only supported by such weak foundations as faith, intuition or experience were thought to be inferior and so were disregarded.

Now, however, Pascal's claim has come into its own. As we saw in the last chapter, we now live in an age where the 'spiritual' is back in fashion. Yes, of course we have not entirely given up on proof, logic and reason. However, at the popular level at least, it's not uncommon, as we've seen, to find belief in such 'irrational' things as spirits, ghosts and fate, as well as a greater appreciation of the spiritual side of life alongside the physical and mental. We are more aware now than we were in the seventeenth century – more even than we were in the 1950s – that we are more than skin and bones, more than a brain in a body, and that subtle, spiritual factors, immune from analysis in a test-tube, determine an awful lot of our experience of life. We know only too well that 'The heart has it reasons, which reason cannot understand.'

We might have expected that this rediscovery of the spiritual was good news for the church. After all, the church has long been the guardian within Western culture of the importance of the spiritual and the numinous. However, as the last chapter indicated, that is not what has happened. The church tends to be associated in many people's minds with 'religion', which is thought of as a very different thing from 'spirituality'. As a result, we get the kind of sporadic commitment to 'God' which we adopt when it suits us but abandon when it doesn't. As a result, the church now finds itself in a surprising place. In the years of 'modernist' rational culture, Christians were used to having their beliefs in God, heaven, angels, souls and the supernatural routinely disdained. Now, however, these are everywhere. The 'religion' sections of bookshops are far more likely to be stocked with 'Mind, Body and Spirit' titles (*Hot Chocolate for the Soul* and the like) than the latest works of Christian theology. The problem is now not that Christianity is too spiritual, but that it is not spiritual enough. This may be a surprising accusation but it is a common one. Church, in the public mind at least, seems to consist of a dreary set of services that offer an encounter with nothing more exciting than a prayer book and a few Victorian hymns – hardly what will get most busy people out of bed on a Sunday morning.

Of course, there are some accusations that the church had better ignore. The criticism that its faith is dull and not spiritual enough is one that Christians do need to hear and take seriously. After all, Christianity does claim to offer an encounter and a relationship with the true God, the maker of heaven and earth. It claims to bring people into contact with him, to know him through his Son Jesus. It has a long and profound mystical tradition – not unquestioned within Christian history, but nonetheless central in various different forms, from catholic to pietist, evangelical and charismatic – which has always claimed that direct experience of the presence and reality of God is possible for us mortals.

By contrast, the God of many churches seems remote. Services can feel like a polite tea party held in Buckingham Palace, where, although you've been invited in, and you know the Queen is in the building, you don't want to disturb her, so you are content to hold the occasion in an ante-room, happy that she's somewhere nearby but rather hoping she won't turn up. Not surprisingly, this tends to imply that church is more about God-the-theory than God-the-person. In one of Nick Hornby's novels, *How to Be Good*, the main character, a doctor called Katie Carr, goes through a mid-life crisis. At one stage it gets so bad that she tries church. Her conclusion (and surely Hornby must have visited a few churches to build his description) is depressingly acute:

> I start to drift off. I have never been to an ordinary service before. I have been to weddings, funerals, christenings, carol services and even harvest festivals, but I have never been to a bog-standard, nobody-there Sunday service. It all feels a long way from God.[1]

If that is what church feels like, 'a long way from God', then it will always have trouble connecting with a culture that is into spirituality. Perhaps the key term is the word 'remote'. That's how it feels. And like it or not, that is the image that many, many people have of church, and that is why they don't come. They yearn for a personal God with whom it might be possible to connect, but they see little evidence (even in the church!) that he might actually exist. And if that's the case, then perhaps the missing ingredient in many churches is a sense of intimacy.

Intimacy with God

We live in a culture starved of intimacy, yet sated with false forms of it. Take two common features of our culture: the cult of celebrity and the obsession with sex. Why are we endlessly fascinated by the lives of the rich and famous? Why do we buy glossy magazines containing trivial detail about where they spend their holidays, who they are seeing and where they shop – especially as all of these are well out of the financial or social reach of most of us. Surely it is at least in part because we desire and need intimacy? We want to feel close to people, to see into their lives, to know their secrets, and in a strange way to feel known by them. Celebrities offer us fake intimacy. We feel we 'know' them, but of course we don't – and worse, they don't know us. The 'stalker' is the warped outcome (or is it the logical extension?) of the cult of celebrity – the person who does not just want to know the intimate details of the famous, but wants to force them to know him too.

And then there is sex. Why is our culture so obsessed with this particular natural human appetite? As C. S. Lewis pointed out years ago, we would think any society which arranged showings of a plate of pork chop, vegetables and gravy, slowly revealed from under a chiffon cloth to sensual music, to be decidedly odd. Yet this is what we do with the human (mainly female) body and our appetite for sex. Douglas Coupland, in his novel *Generation X*, makes a telling point, as one of his characters reflects, 'Starved for affection, terrified of abandonment, I began to wonder if sex was really just an excuse to look deeply into another human being's eyes.'[2] Maybe he is right. Maybe the hunger for sex is really a hunger for intimacy – a hunger for closeness to another person, an experience that for a fleeting moment breaks down the isolation and loneliness of soul that lie hidden behind many a fixed smile. Christians might be tempted to sneer at our preoccupation with sex and celebrity. Yet the longing for intimacy that aches underneath it is in fact a God-given, and ultimately only God-satisfied, desire.

The *different* thing about Jesus compared to any other first-century rabbi was his sense of intimacy with his Father. That is what both intrigued and annoyed people. It fascinated them, so that they searched out this man who seemed to bring God close to them. It also angered those who felt that this sense of intimacy was too daring and presumptuous.[3] Reading the Gospels gives a sense that here is someone who knows the Father's heart, who feels the same compassion, joy, anger and grief that the Father (God-the-person!) feels over his wonderful but suffering creation.

And yet the most surprising aspect of this is that his apprentices are invited and expected to begin experiencing the same encounter. The really shocking thing is not just that Jesus calls God '*Abba*, Father',[4] but that his friends are encouraged to do the same.[5] When he is asked about prayer, his very first lesson, the first line of the model prayer he gives them, teaches them to call God 'Father'. Not 'Almighty God', or 'Divine Architect of the Universe', or 'Great Artificer' – just 'Father in heaven'. All of this means, in terms of New Testament Christology, that Jesus' relationship with the Father is inclusive. On one level, he is the unique Son of God by nature, enjoying a natural intimacy with the Father, which no created being gets near to, as subsequent Christological reflection over the next few centuries made clear. Yet on another level, we are invited by grace to begin to experience and develop that same kind of intimacy with the Father, from whom sin has distanced us. And in a way that is the essence of the exercise. What is the point of Christianity? It is that through Jesus Christ, ordinary, sinful people might be reconciled to the intimacy with God that humanity enjoyed before the fall, when they 'walked with God in the heat of the day' – only this time even better, with a knowledge of just how far God will go to rescue them.

At the heart of Christianity lies the possibility of a restored and transforming relationship with God the Creator, God-the-person. At times in the church's history, this real encounter with God has been shunted off into what is sometimes called the 'mystical tradition', but it has always remained a key part of Christian life and experience over the centuries. From the early desert monks of the fourth and fifth centuries, to the Brethren of the Common Life in the Middle Ages, to the evangelical revival in Europe in the eighteenth century, to charismatic renewal in the twentieth, Christians have constantly gone back to this basic, central factor in Christian life: that God wants to know his people personally – to be in intimate relationship with them day by day. Even the theologians grasped this, whether Augustine in his experience of finding peace at last in his search for God, or Thomas Aquinas' vivid encounter with God at the end of his life which made all his words of theology seem futile in comparison, or Martin Luther's gradual realization that God simply wanted people to trust him, a discovery that changed his life and the course of Western civilization.

It is this personal encounter with God through Christ that lies at the heart of revivals of all kinds of Christianity through the years. It's as if religion has a constant tendency to revert to a bare shell – the outward trappings without the inward core. And time and again, it has to be recalled to its heart. To be sure, at times, Christians have been tempted to go the other way, aiming at a very 'spiritualized' form of religion that dispenses with structures, disciplines or any practical outworking, remaining locked in a spiritual other-worldly realm that never touches real life. But that has, arguably, been less of a problem over the years than the opposite tendency.

In short, there is a need for a much richer theology of the Holy Spirit, as the One who, since Pentecost, brings God's presence to us, and who enables us to respond to God. The Spirit is given to dwell within us in a way that we are meant to notice (John 14:17). A church with a strong doctrine of the Holy Spirit and expectation of his tangible work in the lives of people will seldom convey the idea that God is distant or remote. The Spirit also brings spiritually lifeless hearts, unresponsive to the love and glory of their Creator, into an intimate relationship with the Father (Romans 8:15–16; Galatians 4:6–7). As Augustine pointed out, the Spirit is the bond between the Father and the Son, and he is also the bond between the believer and the Father and the Son. The Spirit brings us into the harmonious and dynamic relationship that lies in the heart of God, and that the doctrine of the Trinity represents. As a result, we are no longer outsiders, but insiders to the nature of God, invited to 'participate in the divine nature' (2 Peter 1:4).

The early church possessed a dynamism which came from their expectation that God was truly with them and working through them in the Spirit, taking their feeble attempts to witness to him, and multi-

plying them through the Spirit. A church without a strong sense of
the Spirit's immediacy, presence and work will tend to convey the
idea that God is bound in history or institutions. A church with a
conviction that the Spirit has been richly (not sparingly) poured out
upon the church (Titus 3:6), and that Christian life is intended to be
one of 'righteousness, peace and joy in the Holy Spirit' (Romans
14:17), will engage with those on the contemporary spiritual search
much more effectively than churches that have largely lost their trust
in the Spirit.

If all this is true, then the idea that church only offers a distant God,
where there is no sense of spiritual encounter with him, is surely a
scandal. It implies that many churches are failing in one of their central
tasks – to enable ordinary people to find a transforming encounter
with God. The churches that will survive and thrive into the future will
be conscious of the need for genuine encounter with God, both
within Christian theology and experience, and within the wider
culture today. They will need to offer and embrace the importance of
experience, the desire for spiritual reality, the hunger for God.

That hunger for God is seldom expressed explicitly *as* a hunger
for God, but breaks out in many different ways today. Even something as mundane as shopping touches on this. As many sociologists
and psychologists have noticed, when we shop, we don't just shop for
things; we shop for meaning. We buy cars, clothes and cosmetics not
just because we need them but because they give shape to our lives.
They say something about us that we want others to hear – that we
are sophisticated, cool, carefree, attractive or whatever. We shop,
therefore, to give meaning and importance to our lives, because we
cannot find it anywhere else. In a way, we shop because we want to
buy transcendence – we want to transcend our 'normal' lives and give
them a significance they wouldn't otherwise have.

The question is whether your church or mine can actually satisfy
that hunger, through both its corporate and individual practices. If
such a person as the doctor in Nick Hornby's novel were to stumble
into your church or mine this coming Sunday morning, would she
creep out again, saying to herself that 'it all felt a long way from
God'? Or would there be something there to draw her back – a sense
that, as St Paul put it when envisaging an outsider calling into church,
'God is really among you!'[6]

Opportunities for intimacy

But what does this mean in practice? There is no one particular form of worship that does the trick. The sense of God's presence cannot be manufactured by clever manipulations of lights, music or digital projectors. However, it makes a huge difference being in a Christian church in which people expect God to show up, where the focus of the gathering is not actually the music group, the songs, the hymns, the minister or even the sermon, but the presence of God himself.

Travelling round to different churches, you quickly get a sense of what really matters in them. There is usually something centre stage. In one kind of church it is the liturgy. There is a fine attention to getting it just right, so that every word, gesture and robe is in place. In others, it is the sermon. Everything else is really just padding, preparation for and afterthoughts to the finely crafted delivery of a 25-minute monologue. In others it is the music – the real heart of the service is the 'time of worship' (what have they been doing up to that point?), where the band swings into action with half an hour of guitar and drums, offering the latest tunes from recently visited Christian festivals, leading to an emotional peak and a subsequent anticlimax.

Now, there is nothing wrong with liturgy, sermons or worship bands. In fact, you might argue that all of them have a vital place in church, to a greater or lesser extent. The problem comes when they take centre stage, which they so often do. There is a huge difference when you sense that, although the same elements are there, the real focus of a gathering of Christians is the presence of God among them. They are gathering not just to say liturgy, to hear a talk or to sing catchy songs, but to pay attention to God – to listen for his voice, to experience his presence in the Spirit and to tune into his agenda for the world.

So it is about expectation. It is about what those who lead worship actually expect to happen, and whether they can lead the people into a sense of the presence of God in the Spirit and then get out of the way. And that may not be the vicar or minister. There may well be others within the church who have this particular gift and who need to be encouraged to use it. Whoever takes the lead, it is a key role of those who lead worship to remind themselves and everyone who is taking part that the focus of this event is not the means (whether music, sermons or liturgy), but the end. And there is only one 'end', God himself. It is also about the expectations of the people who come. If they come expecting only to say a few prayers and listen to a talk during which they will probably drift off, then the whole event is unlikely to be the kind of experience to connect with many of today's spiritual searchers.

This question of enabling intimacy with God is more than just about what happens in Sunday worship, however. It is also about what Christians do day by day, and in particular how (or whether) they are taught to pray. A friend of mine recently began a new business venture. He was not a Christian, although he was very interested in spirituality and wholeness. He was launching a new restaurant and juice bar, with a set of rooms behind it where people could go for classes in various kinds of yoga, Pilates, meditation and the like. The rooms were then rented by a somewhat strange selection of alternative therapists, offering their different wares to all comers. The idea was that people would come for their carrot juice or pasta salad, and then slip into the back for a quick class in Zen meditation before returning to work for the afternoon.

As he described this to me, a thought began to steal into my mind. Why do churches not offer high-profile classes in Christian prayer and meditation, maybe even in settings like this? Might there be a way into Christian faith through the practice of Christian prayer for those who are unlikely to come to listen to a sermon? Would a course in Christian prayer, which included practical training and instruction on the nature of the God to whom we pray, help such a person encounter God for themselves?[7] Might the way into Christian faith, for some people at least, lie in learning to practise it before they come to believe it?

The difficulty would be that we rarely think of the mechanics of prayer, but maybe we should. Usually, prayer is thought of in most churches as something you just 'do'. I have not very often heard sermons or talks describing what you actually do when you pray. I remember a few years ago trying to preach such a sermon myself. I tried to describe what happened in prayer – that you place someone or some situation side by side in your mind with God, and see how that person looks now, seen in the light and presence of God. A fairly experienced Christian in the congregation came up to me afterwards and said that was the first time anyone had ever described to them what you actually do when you pray!

All of us have struggled to pray, to keep concentration, mind from wandering, and wondering if it is all worth it, especially when it comes to silent, contemplative prayer. The point is that this doesn't necessarily come naturally to us. Martin Luther once pointed out:

> No one should depend on his heart and presume to pray without uttering words unless he is well trained in the Spirit and has experience in warding off stray thoughts. Otherwise the devil will thoroughly trick him and soon smother the prayer in his heart. Therefore we should cling to the words and with their help soar upward, until our feathers grow and we can fly without the help of words.[8]

Luther's point is that you start praying by using words others have carefully crafted. To proceed to silent prayer, which simply practises the presence of God, is not something that comes easily. It has to be taught, so that we can progress from one form of prayer to another, so that personal prayer genuinely becomes a vehicle for aligning our wills with God, being assured day after day of his real presence and developing an ongoing sense of intimacy with him.

Too often such vital things as prayer are left as practices we just pick up as we go along. Sermons and instruction contain fine theological dispositions on the importance of prayer, what happens if we don't pray, or why God might or might not answer prayer. Rarely do we find real practical instruction on *how* to pray. Or if we do, it is something extra, for those especially keen on that sort of thing – the quiet contemplatives of the congregation. Yet it was exactly for this reason that the most central and essential Christian prayer was given. Jesus taught his apprentices what we call 'the Lord's Prayer', at least in Luke's version of the story, precisely because they asked him to teach them to pray.[9] Jesus gave them practical lessons in prayer, taught them how to relate to God as Father, and to develop a day-by-day sense of intimacy with God. If it wasn't beneath him to give some simple A–B–C lessons in prayer – even an actual prayer they could say to get them going – why should that seem too simple to us? The spiritually aware searchers of today will find remote church, with a remote God-the-theory, distinctly uninviting. Churches with a clear and practical agenda of enabling people to encounter and connect with 'God-the-person', both corporately and personally, will begin to entice.

Intimacy with others

One of the characteristics of the contemporary search for the spiritual is its individualistic character. Much writing on spirituality, leading towards engagement with yoga, alternative therapy and various kinds of meditation, is essentially about finding personal peace and inner tranquillity. Classes may be run in a group, and exercises practised together, but there is little that is *essentially* communal about it. Its final goal is personal, individual enlightenment or serenity.

Christian spirituality is very different. It is essentially communal. Our need for intimacy goes beyond intimacy with God. Despite what some Christian songs claim, God has made us so that it is simply not true that 'God is all we need'. He has made us to need each other. We are created as social beings, who receive joy, laughter, esteem and significance from God through our relationships with each other. And most importantly, the way in which we are meant to be spiritually formed is in relationship with each other. The fruit of Christian spirituality, the qualities of humility, gentleness, patience, unity and bearing with one another in love (Ephesians 4:2–3), are essentially communal qualities – the characteristics you need to build relationships and community, not primarily to find individual tranquillity. At the very heart of the creation story, we find God as Creator not just of Man, but also of Woman. 'It is not good for the man to be alone,' it says (Genesis 2:18), and that is not just speaking of marriage and relationships between male and female, the central gender polarity of humanity, but of family, friendship and society.

Our culture longs for intimacy – spiritual experience and encounter that reassures us we are not alone in the universe. It also longs for personal relationship that gives us a crucial context for life and growth. That is why so much contemporary 'spirituality' ends up as narcissistic and isolating – because it is individualistic. Our spiritual hunger is met not only in spiritual encounter with God, but also in relationship with other people, through a sense of belonging to something bigger than ourselves, a community involved in asking and answering the big questions that, as we have seen, everyone is still asking.

Does church offer belonging? Nick Hornby's character goes on to describe another aspect of her experience of church:

> The sparsity of the congregation and its apparent lack of interest in anything or anyone, allows us to sit at the back, and pretend we're nothing to do with anything or anybody . . . It feels sad, exhausted, defeated; this may have been the house of God once, you want to tell the handful of people here, but He's clearly moved, shut up shop, gone to a place where there's more of a demand for that sort of thing. And then you look around and you wonder whether the sadness isn't part of the point: those who are able to drag themselves here once a week are not social church-goers, because there's nothing social happening here.

'Nothing social happening here.' If that is true of church, then heaven help us. If church cannot provide a place of belonging, where people can find relationship and intimacy with others, and a place to discover God together, then it is not surprising that people turn elsewhere to find those things. The problem is that in many forms of church life, we think more in terms of attendance than belonging. The measure of church success is attendance. As long as people attend, then we are happy. We turn up on Sundays to 'attend' church, but often the experience offers little in terms of the things that attract real belonging. And in particular it offers little that might make one actually *want* to join. If, as the columnist David Aaronovitch remarks, the respectable church denominations have turned religion into 'a series of mild-mannered social events', then why would anyone want to make this a central part of their week?

The problem is the monopoly of the idea of *congregation* as a synonym for *church*. In 'congregation' mode, most people who are not involved in performing actions up the front wait passively in the pews to be served up something interesting. There is little sense that the people in the pews really matter, or that anything would be missing if one of them didn't turn up one day.

This might mean some radical thinking for church. It may even mean the end of the congregation as we know it. Congregational worship is good for a corporate 'act of worship', but it is lousy for relationship. And that is why the vast majority of growing churches today have a strong small-group network of some kind or another. An increasing number of churches today define 'going to church' not as turning up in a large building on a Sunday morning at 10.30, but as going to a home on a Thursday evening, where they gather around a table, surrounded by eight or nine other people, to whom they are profoundly committed and in whose lives they are deeply involved. Or alternatively, it may consist of a commitment to a group of Christians gathered around a joint activity, a workplace or a network of friends. And these gatherings are not just for an abstract discussion of sections of the Bible, or stilted prayer. Instead, they try to build spiritual friendship, to tell each other about how the week has been with a level of honesty found only in places where there is trust and confidentiality, to bring all that before God in thoughtful, perceptive prayer for each other, to confess failure and sin, to plan how they can (maybe together with other local groups) make a difference for good in their local area, and how they might attract others into the life of Christ they are experiencing together.[10]

That is increasingly many people's experience of church. It appeals because it offers the very thing that more familiar versions lack, and that Nick Hornby's doctor failed to find – a sense of intimacy and belonging.

We might explain this by the idea that some older models of church are like a restaurant. When you go to a restaurant, everything is done for you. You sit at your table, make your choice from the menu and wait patiently. Someone else cooks the meal, delivers it to your place, asks you if you're enjoying it, takes away the used plates, and does the washing up. You just pay up and leave. Too often church is like that, only a bit less tasty. It is all dependent on just a few people who do the work, and everyone else remains essentially passive throughout. If those people (usually the vicar/minister, churchwardens, deacons, readers etc.) didn't turn up, then the whole thing would fall apart. If the people in the pews didn't turn up, nothing much would change at all.

Another image for church, however, might be a 'bring and share' supper. In this kind of meal, the arrangement is very different. Here, everyone brings something to share with everyone else. Someone brings some salad, someone else brings chicken, and someone else brings potatoes or ham. The event only works if everyone brings something, and they all bring something different. If someone fails to bring their pot of food, then the whole event is a little poorer, but it would still happen anyway.

Church that expects a few people to do the tasks that really matter, and everyone else to sit passively, will not tend to generate a strong sense of belonging. When it doesn't really matter whether you are there or not, it becomes an incentive not to bother. On the other hand, the kind of church experience which means that everyone is expected both to give and receive, where there is a high value placed on mutual support and participation, despite perhaps initially being more demanding, actually will encourage a greater sense of belonging and commitment, and a deeper communal spirituality.

Religion or spirituality?

This chapter has argued that in the face of a tangible distaste for religion, and a corresponding hunger for spiritual reality, even if that is vague and nebulous, church will need to return to one of its core reasons for existing – to invite ordinary people into relationship with an extraordinary God. It will need to take seriously the need to offer intimacy – intimacy with God and intimacy with other people – a communally experienced and learnt spirituality.

At the same time, the church would be very foolish to throw out babies with bathwater. The popular distinction between religion (bad) and spirituality (good), which emerged time and time again in the research for this book, does need to be questioned. In our culture, spirituality is usually seen as dealing with the inner life, some kind of internal tranquillity, a personal aura or glow that guards you from the harmful things that might happen in ordinary life. However, as Rowan Williams has argued, religion is decidedly 'material'. It involves a set of specific bodily practices, such as kneeling for prayer, going to a particular building at certain times, habits of life that make you into a sign within this world of something beyond it.[11] That is how Christian spirituality is expressed – in physical, bodily actions. It is not purely an inner private thing, but is in fact very public. Religion is something you do, not just believe or feel, and it's important in our thinking about the need for a greater spiritual tone to contemporary church life not to forget the outward expression of religious practice. Practices like public prayer, speaking about faith to those who aren't

Christians, the wearing of crosses or WWJD ('What Would Jesus Do?') bracelets, performing actions that become signs of the kingdom of God, are all vital. Otherwise, Christianity becomes a privatized spiritual experience that loses the power to subtly and subversively change the way communities work or people behave.

If contemporary Christianity is to be truly spiritual, in the sense of animating (and not shunning) the bodily and the physical, then it must be a material, public, visible thing. That way it can become more spiritual, more real and more influential than the sometimes rather precious and self-absorbed types of spirituality so often found in Western societies today.

Notes to Chapter 2

1. Nick Hornby, *How to Be Good* (Penguin, 2001).
2. Douglas Coupland, *Generation X: Tales for an Accelerated Culture* (Abacus, 1992), p. 30.
3. Read John 8:30–59 for an encounter that demonstrates this dynamic perfectly.
4. Mark 14:36.
5. St Paul understood this too. See also Romans 8:15; Galatians 4:6.
6. 1 Corinthians 14:25.
7. See Rob Frost, *Essence* (Kingsway, 2002), for an attempt to do something along these lines.
8. *Luther's Works* (Fortress Press, 1981, 42:25).
9. Luke 11:1ff.
10. For more on this kind of vision of church see Howard Astin, *Body and Cell: Making the Transition to Cell Church: A First Hand Account* (Monarch Books, 2002); Michael Green (ed.), *Church without Walls: A Global Examination of Cell Church* (Paternoster, 2002); Phil Potter, *The Challenge of Cell Church: Getting to Grips with Cell Church Values* (Bible Reading Fellowship, 2001); Pete Ward, *Liquid Church* (Paternoster, 2002).
11. Rowan Williams, Romanes Lecture, Oxford University, 18 November 2004. See http://www.archbishopofcanterbury.org/sermons_speeches/041118.html.

SECTION 2 | **CHRISTIANITY**

While belief in God is widespread, specific Christian claims are treated as rather less credible. Yet much disbelief is both superficial and tentative, more shaped by personal experience and cultural norms than by careful thought. This hesitant disbelief requires a humble style of apologetics, which is alert and responsive to personal experience, cultural trends and popular genres.

3. INCREDIBLE CLAIMS

If the general level of spiritual and theistic belief remains stubbornly high in Britain, and the level of church attendance (see Chapter 7) low, the level of belief in specific Christian claims hovers somewhere in between. People neither know nor believe as much Christian doctrine as they did fifty years ago, but rather more believe than attend church on any given week.

When the research company ORB surveyed people's beliefs for the BBC programme *Soul of Britain* in 2000, they found that 38% of people said they believed Jesus was the 'Son of God'. This compared with 26% who said they thought he was 'just a man' and 25% who thought he was 'just a story'. The same survey reported that 23% thought the Bible was 'the unique word of God', 28% thought that it was 'another holy book like others', 20% that 'it consists of moral tales/ nice stories only' and 9% that 'it is not longer relevant to our culture'.

Levels of belief in the resurrection are harder to pinpoint, as it is far from clear whether interviewees in surveys understand the Christian concept of resurrection, frequently confusing it with the idea of life after death. When the ORB/*Soul of Britain* study examined this belief, it reported that 51% of people said they believed in life after death and 32% in 'the resurrection of the dead', whilst a survey for *Reader's Digest* in 2005 found that 58% of people believe in an 'afterlife'.

On the resurrection of Christ, a survey conducted for the *Fortean Times* in 2001 found that a third of people believed the biblical account of the resurrection, a figure similar to that reported by the European Values study in 1990, whereas another study two years later reported 47% claiming to believe that Christ rose from the dead, whilst 36% said they did not.

The ORB/*Soul of Britain* survey reported that 52% of people claimed to believe in heaven and 28% in hell, whilst the ICM survey for the BBC programme 'What the world thinks of God' found 54% of people agreeing with the statement 'I don't believe death is the end.'

These figures might surprise us. If as many people believe what they claim to believe in these surveys, why don't they do anything about it? Is it not rather strange to believe that Christ was raised from the dead or that death is not the end, yet never to darken the door of a church (or any other religious building), as somewhere between a quarter and a third of people appear to do?

This apparent disconnection makes more sense when we consider the context of these beliefs. Firstly, levels of knowledge are very low. It is one thing saying that you believe Jesus was the Son of God. It is quite another knowing what that might actually mean and how it affects you. In this way, surprisingly high levels of belief in Christian doctrine are blunted and, more importantly, made rather irrelevant. Having said that, such ignorance also blunts the edge of disbelief, as we shall see below.

Secondly, beliefs are embedded in lives and lifestyles. Much as we like to pretend otherwise, human beings are not perfectly balanced, logical and rational thinking machines, free from physical, emotional or spiritual influences – but instead 'animated bodies', whose beliefs and thoughts are profoundly shaped by who, where and when they are.

Both of these contexts – of ignorance and experience – can be seen at work in people's most powerful objections to Christianity. These objections themselves call the church to the task of apologetics, but in understanding the contexts that influence the way they are felt and expressed, that task is made subtly different.

Suffering and the goodness of God

When ORB asked people in 2000 why they thought some people didn't believe in God, the most common response, at 41%, was 'There is too much suffering, poverty and injustice in the world for God to exist.' This finding was supported, from a different perspective, in the ICM/BBC 'What the world thinks of God' poll four years later, which found that people in the UK had a greater problem with God and suffering than those in any other country interviewed.[1] In the UK 52% of respondents agreed with the statement 'I find it hard to believe in God/ a higher power when there is so much suffering in the world,' whilst 46% disagreed.

As has long been recognized, the Christian belief in an omnipotent and benevolent God in the face of human suffering is the biggest barrier to commitment to Christianity. At its worst, it is claimed, not only does Christianity fail to answer the painful question of suffering, but, in so far as it has been involved in religious wars and conflicts across the world, it has actually made the problem worse. A loveless, purposeless, Godless universe is a bleak and miserable prospect, but at least it is one in which suffering is not an anomaly. God, let alone the all-loving, all-powerful God of Christian doctrine, makes the issue of suffering all the more acute, with the evil done in his name by fanatical followers redoubling the problem.

For some interviewees, usually those whose existing anti-Christian sentiments were very clear, this problem was enough to condemn God, Christianity, Christians and the church without any leave to appeal. For others, in an example of how cultural context influenced intellectual questions, the problem of suffering was intensified by being viewed, albeit unconsciously, through consumerist eyes. God's silence in the area of suffering, when seen through consumer eyes, became a cosmic example of bad service provision, provoking real hostility on occasion:

> You pick the phone up and it's a friend who has some sad news . . . I'm talking about personal experiences. There's nobody up there and if there is he's basically downright uncaring.

Still other discussions of suffering were less angry and more nuanced, beginning with the usual premises – 'If there is a God, why are all those horrible things happening?' – and then being refined by various counter-arguments. Some interviewees suggested that we should not reasonably expect to live in Elysian bliss – 'It can't all have been good . . . No, it can't be . . . We have to see suffering'; whilst others reckoned that God could not be credibly blamed for human evils. 'People die hungry,' one middle-aged man reasoned, 'and that's probably because the governments aren't investing or the money is going elsewhere on arms.' Such disasters 'man makes himself'. Blaming them on God was little more than hypocrisy.

It was also hypocritical to blame God for life's pains and not to thank him for its joys. 'You always seem to ask the question when things are going wrong for you "Why me?"' one young man commented. 'But when things are going all right, you never seem to think, "Oh well, I'm the lucky one."'

In response to these modifications, most people agreed that God was culpable for most natural disasters, except perhaps those for which human environmental degradation was responsible. All the interviews were conducted some time before the 2004 Boxing Day tsunami killed a quarter of a million people around the Indian Ocean, but the sentiments expressed were of a piece with many of the reactions to that disaster:

> If God created the world, why does he allow things like earthquakes and famines and droughts and natural disasters to happen? Not man-made disasters, I mean – things like wars man creates for himself – but natural disasters, why does he allow them to happen?

However people's discussions about suffering proceeded, and almost irrespective of whether accusations or counter-arguments convicted or acquitted God, it was clear that suffering was not simply an intellectual problem. Instead, it was, first and foremost, a personal and emotional issue. Debates about theodicy were grounded in actual experience. People engaged with the question of suffering, at least initially, on an intimate, personal level. The big philosophical questions about suffering were approached through personal disaster or family tragedy or social breakdown or global injustice. To that end, no *argument*, no matter how brilliant or subtle, could have had any significant impact on people's thoughts. A more suitable response might have been a hug.

Science and the credibility of God

Science has historically, in the popular mind at least, ranked close behind suffering as a reason not to believe basic Christian claims. Those who view Christianity as a primitive scientific theory see its credibility as having been damaged by Galileo and destroyed by Darwin, a view aided by those Christians who insist we must choose between Genesis and evolution.

Science was seen as a reason not to believe by many of the people interviewed for this book, although the specific reasons offered were disappointingly weak, often amounting to little more than the fact that there were no dinosaurs in the Bible. Several people claimed that 'Christians say that the world was made in six or seven days,' which left too many questions unanswered. 'Where in that six days were the dinosaurs made? And when did they get wiped out?' one interviewee asked.

One young man claimed that science had disproved 'miracles', and hence disproved those religions that based themselves on miracles, although the example he gave to support this view was rather unfortunate:

> You've got the Turin Shroud, haven't you, where scientists are now saying that that couldn't possibly have been the robe that Jesus was buried with. So that is down to science again, isn't it?

Oddly enough, evolutionary theory, the weapon that you would have most expected hostile interviewees to attack Christianity with, was often as problematic as its supposed alternative. Not only was the evolutionary process itself a rather late arrival on the cosmic scene, but the world seemed to fit together too well to be a 'fluke'. 'It just seems to be so well designed,' one middle-aged woman said. 'I don't see how that can just happen out of a random explosion in space. It just seems too fantastic.'

The absence of substantive, specific examples to justify their view that science disproves Christianity did not prevent a number of interviewees from insisting that this was still the case, however. In reality, many of those people who viewed science as a barrier to belief did so for cultural rather than intellectual reasons.

Without realizing it, they had bought into the controlling 'warfare' metaphor for understanding the relationship between science and Christianity. This metaphor gained popularity in the later nineteenth century when, after the publication of Darwin's *Origin of Species* and the subsequent controversy, several partisan historians wrote books charting the relationship between science and religion over the centuries. These used the concept of an ongoing and bitter war as the controlling metaphor – that is, the image by means of which people might understand an otherwise long, complex and abstract relationship. 'Science' and 'religion' had been enemies since the time of the Renaissance and, consequently, in evaluating them, one must choose between them.

Despite having been subsequently discredited by most historians of science, this metaphor remains the silently dominant, if not quite exclusive one in the popular mind today. As one middle-aged man intimated, it was either Darwinism or Christianity: 'I'd rather believe Charles Darwin than the Bible, when it comes to how the world was made.'

The result of this was that *anything* that indicated that science and religion are different, such as the fact that they have different methods, aim at different objectives, or deal with different considerations, could be taken as proof that they are antagonistic. Indeed, simply by using the category-words 'science' and 'religion', people were reinforcing the idea that the two were irreconcilably different. Science is a barrier to religious belief because science is science and religion is religion.

Hence, when asked to explain *why* science is a barrier to religious faith, interviewees' responses tended not to cite the specific details of the science–theology interface. Instead, they referred to the fact that, for example, science is an ongoing enterprise in discovery ('People find out more through science and are still finding out more through science than they do [through] religion'), or that science has proved a highly effective explanatory mechanism ('We know how the world began and questions . . . about the creation theory and all these other things'), or that science has achieved a great deal ('With science you see a lot . . . you see the science of people having babies through IVF and things like that'). None of these statements was in itself untrue but none actually explained why science should be a barrier to religious belief.

In much the same way, and perhaps more significantly, because science supposedly demands proof, so should religion.[2] Unless faith adopted the standards of science and became provable (and thereby, of course, stopped being faith), it was always going to be unsatisfactory. One middle-aged woman said, 'I'd like to believe in God because of the comfort aspect, but I don't because there's not enough scientific basis for it,' and another remarked, 'I don't say that I don't believe . . . [but] until a proof has been shown to me . . . there's too many missing links.'

In this way, science, traditionally thought to be a barrier (for some) to Christian belief and therefore an important area for apologetic engagement, was shown still to be just such a barrier, but for cultural and contextual reasons just as much as scientific or theological ones.

Historical reliability and revelation of God

Although the popular level of biblical knowledge is lower today than perhaps at any time since the Reformation, the people interviewed were clearly aware of the importance and centrality of the Bible to the Christian faith. They also believed that to cast doubts over biblical claims was to erode the very foundations of Christianity.

In the same way as scientific ignorance precluded any detailed objection to Christianity in that area, the low level of biblical or historical knowledge precluded any substantive or detailed theological objections. The few that were raised, like the Genesis/evolution example given above, were not persuasive. A few people claimed that the Bible was self-contradictory, but were unable to offer an explanation any more specific than the idea that 'Matthew, Mark, Luke and John' contained the 'same stories' and that there 'are four different stories in there as well'.

In a slightly different approach, one interviewee claimed that the God of the Old Testament was very different from that of the New. 'I understand there to be two basic concepts of God which are revealed through the Bible,' he said. 'The Old Testament God being the creator, wrath, torturing people like the book of Job, and then you have the New Testament version of painting God as a father or shepherd looking after his flock.' This might not have proved the Bible wrong as such, but it certainly suggested that it was inconsistent and untrustworthy.

For the vast majority of interviewees, their level of biblical knowledge was too low – sometimes breathtakingly low, as when one person asked whether *War and Peace* was 'part of the Bible', and another said that the Bible was 'like *Lord of the Rings* . . . all about another universe, a Middle Earth' – to offer any specific objections. This did not, however, prevent those people who voiced an opinion on the subject from declaring things like, 'There is no evidence to support anything in the Bible,' or even more aggressively, that 'It's probably just a book written by a silly old man who thought, "Oh, this would be good."'

The primary reason for this was the near-universal belief that the Bible had been written down centuries after the events it describes, after having been passed through a long and increasingly unreliable chain of witnesses. This was, in other words, the Chinese Whispers theory, in which either details were slowly changed by poor memory or, more ominously, 'stories were [intentionally] exaggerated with the telling'.

This Chinese Whispers theory was given further, crucial support by the subtle cultural context that cast aspersions on anything that was old. Interviewees, of whatever age, liked to see themselves as living within, and indeed being on the cutting edge of, a tough, sceptical age. Naïvety was a terrible charge that was readily laid at the door of those who lived in the past, a past that need not be very distant. Indeed, it need only be a few decades ago. 'Older generations . . . were perhaps brought up not to question things so much,' one woman in her early twenties said. 'People question things more now than they used to,' a middle-aged man echoed. 'If you were told [then] that black was white, you believed it.' 'Old' frequently implied not just antiquated and irrelevant, but also naïve or unreliable.

If people of two generations ago could be judged credulous, it was hardly surprising that the opinions of those who lived two thousand years ago were treated with considerable disbelief. In a pre-modern, pre-scientific age, people did not exercise the scepticism that enables us today to ascertain truth. Even more than that, 'Back then there wasn't such things as the media,' one young man reasoned, 'so [news] wasn't as widespread [and] people didn't know about it as much' (which, incidentally, was the first time I as researcher had ever heard an interviewee claiming that the media made things *more* reliable). How, in short, could you possibly believe anything that was that old?

Interestingly, as soon as the historicity of the Bible had been undermined, biblical stories could be reappropriated and even be praised, according to particular preferences. Once biblical veracity had been disproved, people could smile warmly on the Bible, saying things like, 'I think it has a lot of truth in it,' or 'It's a lovely story and children love it,' or (most damningly) 'Some people believe these stories are true and some people don't think they are true but they are nice stories.'

Similarly, once the need to respond to the life-challenging words and deeds of Christ had been obviated by the Chinese Whispers theory, people could and did speak warmly of his wisdom, love and humanity. It was almost as if, once biblical stories had been neutered, they could be brought back into the fold, all fear of them impregnating vulnerable minds with their 'false' ideas gone.

The other contextual consideration that influenced people's attitude to the Bible was that of ignorance about genres. All but a tiny minority of people understood the Bible as a single, monolithic, indivisible text. Accordingly, few had any idea of the range of styles and genres within it, believing it to be an advice book or rule book of some kind, or a biography or history book, or perhaps a story book – a term that was usually used to undermine its veracity rather than to describe its genre.

A small number of biblical books and stories were mentioned by name, but there was little idea that they should be read or treated differently, and those Christians who attempted to do so were sometimes accused of sophistry. 'The problem I have with the Bible', one middle-aged woman said, 'is which bits they take literally and which bits they say, "Oh no, that's just a fable and the moral of that story is . . ." Oh, come on, you can't have it both ways.'

The result was that the historical credibility of Jesus, Mary and Peter could be equated with that of Adam, Eve and Noah, because the Gospels were not necessarily any different from the early chapters of Genesis. Ignorance concerning genre worked alongside scepticism towards the past in providing the context in which people treated the Bible as a barrier to Christian faith, often in spite of their superficial biblical knowledge. As with science, the problem was as much cultural as it was intellectual.

Other religions and the uniqueness of God
A fourth major objection to Christian belief was the idea that Christianity might be uniquely true. The ICM survey for the BBC programme 'What the world thinks of God' asked respondents whether they agreed with the statement 'My God is the only true God.' In the UK 31% of people agreed with this – less than in any other country surveyed and compared to 51% in the US, 78% in Mexico and 96% in Indonesia. Conversely, and not surprisingly, 65% disagreed with the statement in the UK, more than in any of the other nine countries asked.

Despite the fact that the same survey recorded that 42% of Britons claimed to have 'studied religious texts', closer research made it clear that people's response to the statement about uniqueness of beliefs was due more to the cultural context of omnitolerance than to theological analysis.

The most substantive reason for rejecting claims of uniqueness was that other religions made the same claims. People commonly said things like, 'If there's only one God, why the hundreds of religions?' or 'Some religions say that their God made the earth and then Christianity says their God made the earth, and you know someone's got to be lying,' and left it at that.

Underlying this reason, however, was the rather more pressing need to foster and demonstrate tolerance. Tolerance, as we shall see in Chapter 5, was the unquestioned supreme value in most people's moral universe and, accordingly, intolerance was the greatest sin. Those social groups deemed to be intolerant were, somewhat paradoxically, not to be tolerated. Few claims were considered to be more intolerant that the religious claim that 'My God is the only God,' as such an attitude invariably led, in many people's minds, to conflict and bloodshed. Christianity's claim to uniqueness, itself not fully understood, was a barrier to belief not because it was demonstrably untrue but because it was culturally unacceptable.

Overall, the research showed that whilst the majority of people

who stood between the extremes of convinced atheism and convinced theism could be described as vaguely and nervously theistic –
prepared to accept the likelihood of an abstract but irrelevant God
but more hesitant about the existence of the meaningful, personal
God whom they actually wanted to exist – they had more problems
with the particular claims of the Christian faith.

Those that were most problematic – God's omnipotence and
benevolence, his credibility and his uniqueness – naturally related to
those intellectual problems that have long been areas for apologetic
engagement. For a range of sometimes sophisticated but more often
superficial reasons, suffering, science, history and the existence of
other faiths were commonly thought to invalidate core Christian
claims.

Yet, time and again, what emerged when speaking to people about
these issues was not the intellectual problem itself, important as this
could be, but the way in which it was founded on and shaped by
other, often invisible, cultural trends. Whether it was the warfare
metaphor that controlled people's understanding of the relationship
between science and religion, or the attitude towards the past that
undermined the very idea of biblical reliability, or the tendency
toward 'totalitolerance' that meant claims of religious uniqueness
were simply unacceptable, the social and cultural currents in which
people lived heavily influenced them and what they (thought they)
knew. All this points towards the continuing need for apologetics, but
for an apologetics that is alert to the concerns of twenty-first-century
Britain.

Notes to Chapter 3

1. Countries that, incidentally, included India, Nigeria, Lebanon and
   Mexico.
2. The philosophy of science recognizes that the question of scientific
   falsification/verification is far more complex than this statement allows,
   but that fact was not mentioned in a single interview.

4. HUMBLE APOLOGETICS

In 2004, the philosopher Anthony Flew announced that after a life-time of public atheism, he now believed in God. But he was at pains to point out that this was theism, not Christianity. The Christian God was a step too far. Flew's God 'could be a person in the sense of a being that has intelligence and a purpose, I suppose', but he was certainly not specific and interactive with the world, as the Bible says God is. Flew was theistic, but not Christian.

He is not alone. Holding belief in a God, but remaining unconvinced by more personal, Christian understandings of God, describes many in contemporary society, as Chapters 1 and 3 have indicated. All this gives Christians some cause for hope and at the same time might make them take a deep breath. There is a job to be done.

One recent survey asking church members why they felt churches in the UK and Ireland are failing found that 73% of the respondents cited the impression that there seemed to be few good reasons to believe.[1] In particular they bemoaned the inability of Christian leaders and clergy to give good reasons for faith. One elderly Yorkshireman in the survey put it with typical bluntness: 'After 50 years of going to church I gradually realised it was all nonsense.' If such people cannot find answers to their growing questions about Christian faith, then it is not surprising that the church haemorrhages members year after year.

On the one hand, the research presented here highlights how many people there are who genuinely would like to believe. It seems that many would quite like there to be a personal God to believe in, to turn to at times of despair or loneliness, or simply as an ear to hear the instinctive prayers that most of us utter from time to time. There is a wistfulness in the words of the person who said:

> The world would be very peaceful if everyone followed him. There would be no war, no hunger, no hatred . . . [God is] someone you call upon if you are in distress or when you haven't got anyone else to talk to.

The problem is not an inbuilt suspicion of the supernatural or outright hostility to the idea of God in itself, but rather the difficulties in believing what (people think) Christianity expects them to believe.

These findings also point to the fact that there are a number of genuine difficulties, whether objections or misunderstandings, which prevent many people from taking Christianity seriously. The big questions of life, purpose, meaning and suffering do still get asked, and the take-up on Alpha and other enquiry courses (in a way regardless of the numbers who actually become Christians on them) continues to emphasize this very point – that people do want to ask big questions, but don't always know where and how to do it. And if they ask big questions, they might be willing to listen to some answers, if Christians are able to provide them in the right place and the right way.

There are perhaps two related issues here. One is that there is a high level of ignorance about Christian faith. The other is that there are a number of quite specific, persistent and very common arguments or objections that prevent many people from believing Christian claims. It is as if these objections provide an automatic and involuntary force field defending the territory against God so that whenever the question of God arises, so do these nagging questions whispering in the ear of the unbeliever that this thing cannot really be taken seriously. So how can Christians today address this twin challenge – what we might call the intellectual test of faith today?

Answering back

All of this brings us to the role of the branch of Christian theology known as 'apologetics'. Of course, apologetics is not as it might seem, the science of how to apologize for one's faith as often or profusely as possible. It actually comes from a Greek word, *apologia*, which normally referred to a speech in defence of something. Apologetics is the defence of Christianity in the public square against those who would misrepresent or attack it.

Perhaps the golden era of Christian apologetics was in the second century AD. It became a major weapon in the Christian armoury during the early years of the church as it began to get a hearing in the hostile pagan environment of the Roman Empire. As more people heard of the Christians, and rumours spread about what they did and didn't do, Christian apologists such as Justin Martyr, Athenagoras and Tatian wrote public defences of Christianity. These documents tried, on the one hand, to counter some of the arguments used by contemporary Greek philosophers against the church; and, more positively, to explain the real nature of the faith and distinguish it from the false reports that were common at the time. At the start of the fourth century, however, when Constantine became the first Christian ruler of the Roman Empire, Christianity became respectable, and quickly moved to centre stage as the pivotal and uniting ideology of the Graeco-Roman world. As a result, the pagan critique of Christianity soon faded. After the third century, there weren't too many critics of standard, orthodox Christianity around any more. Apologetics seemed less necessary. Now, we are back at square one. The Christian church now finds itself increasingly as a minority opinion in Europe at least, often criticized, misunderstood or even disdained both in public and private. Maybe the time for apologetics has come again.

Anxious about apologetics?

For some years now, Christians have discussed among themselves the realities of living in a 'postmodern' world – in fact, it's probably true to say that at the popular level at least, postmodernism has been discussed more in Christian circles than anywhere else. A standard line taken in such conversations suggests that the days of apologetics are over. The argument goes that postmodern people are no longer interested in whether Christianity is true; they want to know only if it works. In other words, they are no longer concerned about questions of objective truth; they simply want a pragmatic solution that helps them get through life relatively smoothly and effectively. And Christians wanting to commend Christian faith have started to suggest, therefore, that the key task today is not so much to show that Christianity is true, but to show that it works.

Apologetics also comes in for critique in some Christian circles for a number of other more ideological or theological reasons as well. If you can never argue someone into faith, why bother trying in the first place? Again, apologetics can seem like trying to justify God by appeal to some higher rules of logic or independent standards of rationality that are the sole arbiters of whether something is true or false. Some theologians or philosophers have pointed out the obvious problem with this – how can you appeal to anything higher than God himself? Surely God does not have to justify himself by our standards of what we can or cannot prove to be true.

A similar objection is simply that God is not susceptible to proof. Trying to prove the existence of God is like trying to prove the existence of love or describe the smell of coffee – even if you could do it, it wouldn't get you very far until you had actually experienced it. Therefore what we need to do is get people to experience God, not to prove him. Then again, others will say that an attempt to convince someone intellectually of the truth of Christianity is usurping the role of the Spirit. It is God who brings someone to a living faith, not human rational argument.

Now, all of these objections to apologetics have some merit. And they certainly raise big questions about certain kinds of apologetics, as we'll see. However, as we've seen in the research presented here, people who don't believe do sometimes give reasons for why they don't believe. They still ask the big questions, expecting there to be some kind of plausible answers from religious people if they are to believe in God, let alone trust him.

As a background to all this, Christians will indeed have to work hard at showing that Christianity works in practice, demonstrating the genuineness and uniqueness of their faith through a Christian lifestyle that is strikingly distinctive.[2] However, they still have to answer those questions when they are asked. Again, vital as it is to encourage people into a genuine experience of the real, live God who is out there, questions will inevitably arise as to how they interpret those experiences. You might have a dramatic encounter with spiritual reality at a worship service, but how do you know whether that is God or just hypnotic auto-suggestion or the result of cleverly manipulated emotion? You can be overwhelmed by the beauty of a sunset or the awesomeness of space, but again, is that God? Or is it just an experience of wonder at the physical world, leading more properly to nature worship rather than Christian faith? The questions keep coming up and need answers.

Christians still need to think about what they say to the questions they are asked, how to address the difficulties and arguments that stop other people believing. So it may be that apologetics is still necessary – arguably more so as Christian faith becomes less prominent in public discourse and less well known by the average person. There are also good theological reasons why this venture is necessary.

As the Word became flesh in Jesus, it took form in a specific time and place and culture. It inevitably addressed both the people and the patterns of thought it encountered. It was expressed in human language and concepts, and used imagery and ideas from the marketplace of ideas in the first century. It also had to try to overcome the misconceptions of those who misunderstood it, raised arguments against it and found it bizarre. And it did this without compromising its true nature as God's truth, embodied in his world. Apologetics also takes for granted that people created by God have an inbuilt restlessness for him – Pascal's 'God-shaped hole' at the heart of human experience; albeit one that is stilled and distracted by sin. In short, it takes seriously God's gracious approach to us in Christ, in language and cultural forms we can understand, and our status as created beings, with a capacity to relate to God. However, it may be that what we need is a different kind of apologetics than we are used to.

A different style

Some time ago I got into a theological discussion with one of my students. He came to find me after something I'd said in a lecture and basically wanted to pick a fight with me. He planted himself in my room and was clearly not willing to leave until he had argued me into submission and I had admitted that I was wrong. With the coolness of hindsight, I can now see that his point of view had some merit. However, the more he argued, the less I wanted to give in. It became a battle of wills. The more he pressed me, the more aggressive he became, the less I wanted to back down. It wasn't exactly mature or wise of me to react that way but I couldn't help it. We've all been in discussions like that, when the truth or falsehood of an argument becomes irrelevant in a sheer battle of cerebral skill where victory goes, not to the one who has the truth, but to the one who can play the game best and outwit his opponent with deft intellectual footwork.

If we're honest, Christian apologetics has often been conducted in this way. The purpose appears to be to argue unbelievers into submission by showing them the falsehood of their position and forcing them to back down. The result is that often the battle is won and the war lost. The loser simply comes back more determined than ever to bolster an opinion with stronger arguments in future. Now this may work with some people. It may work with those for whom rational, logical argument is the main way to make decisions, manage life and run relationships. The problem is that those people are relatively scarce. Most of us are driven more by instinct, impression and desire than logic. The other difficulty with it is that if you can argue someone into faith, you can also argue them out of it. Such an approach is very susceptible to the changing of intellectual fashions, or to people with greater rhetorical skill than the Christian apologist.

Moreover, the research in this book shows pretty conclusively that if there's one thing average persons don't take to, it is someone forcing their views upon them. That doesn't, of course, disallow argument, but it does make us think hard about *how* such argument is conducted – the manner of our apologetics will be as important as its content. The purpose of Christian apologetics cannot be to prove God or browbeat anyone into intellectual submission. Instead, it must have a more modest, humble but still vital role in Christian interaction with a sceptical culture.

John Stackhouse suggests that apologetics has three distinct but related aims.[3] Firstly, it exists to remove obstacles to faith.

Christianity is seen by many people as inherently sexist, simplistic, homophobic or irrelevant. If so, it will need to be presented in a way that overcomes these perceptions and sheds a more positive light on the faith. The aim will be to show that it is not as problematic in these areas as it may seem, and if it does take up particular positions on these matters, there are good reasons for doing so.

The second aim is to clarify issues. If someone says they do not believe in God, a useful question in response might be, 'Which God don't you believe in?' Quite often that question elicits a picture of God that no Christian would want to believe in either, opening the way for a more positive conversation about the God whom Christians do believe in and trust. In other words, apologetics helps to clarify the questions and statements that people make about Christian faith. It can enable them to discard unhelpful ways of approaching it, and it can suggest more useful ways of trying to understand what Christians are trying to commend. It simply provides for a better, more fruitful, conversation.

The third aim, Stackhouse suggests, is to offer inducements to believe. Christians do believe that if anyone chooses to taste and see, they will discover that the Lord is good. If so, then they will want to explain and extend those attractions to those who have always thought religion was a devious plot to stop anyone enjoying life – a combination of hair shirts and humiliation.

Now these three aims for Christian apologetics deliberately do not include the winning of rational arguments. Neither do they allow for any kind of attempt to prove the existence of God or aggressive tactics to make a fool of anyone who doesn't believe in Jesus. Of course, it is only the Holy Spirit who can bring someone to life spiritually. A classic Christian theology of the Holy Spirit would tell us that unless the Spirit enables us, we are simply incapable of responding to God on our own. And that is because, as the great St Augustine argued, we can only know God if we learn to love him, not by trying to understand him. The key question is not what we think but whom we love, and 'argument cannot produce affection'.[4] Christians will want to try to coax those who want to believe, those who are 'nervously theistic', into a clearer understanding of Christianity so that the Spirit can do his work in their hearts and minds. Apologetics that tries to remove obstacles, clarify issues and offer inducements doesn't tread on holy ground, trying to do the Spirit's work for him. Instead, it simply 'prepares the way of the Lord' into the frail, tentative, human hearts of the unconvinced.

The postmodern aversion to apologetics has a point. We live in a culture that is much less open to claims to truth, much more pre-pared to question anything that claims to come with the authority of age or God or tradition. The apologetics needed in such a culture will need to be humble, not trying to claim too much too soon, nor to claim more than it can deliver, but instead, seeking gently to drop those things into conversation that will intrigue, clarify and explain. It will often come in the form of questions rather than statements, as it often did in the mouth of Jesus. And above all it will need to be done out of a desire for the well-being of the whole persons addressed, a sense that they are loved by God as they are, rather than any sense of winning victories in argumentation.

New genres

Besides a different style, apologetics in the context of the culture por-trayed by this research will also need to explore different methods. Apologetics might seem wordy and dull. When you think of apolo-getics and apologists, you might tend to think of brainy people producing speeches or books that are carefully argued and highly cerebral. The problem is that the vast majority of the population in Britain today, unless they are in full-time education, would never listen to anyone giving a lengthy talk (let alone a Christian), nor would they pick up a Christian book by choice. These are media which, whether we like it or not, are unlikely to achieve the widespread change of attitude that Christians may want, correcting misunder-standings and offering Christian answers to the big questions of destiny, purpose, suffering and the spiritual realm.

One of the most popular books of recent times is Dan Brown's *The Da Vinci Code*. The book runs to around 600 pages, yet reached Amazon.com's coveted number-one spot, has been the number-one seller in both the US and the UK, and lasted 47 weeks in the *New York Times*'s bestsellers list. It is a fast-moving, brilliantly told story of deception, conspiracy, murder and intrigue. It is controversial in Christian circles because it puts forward the theory that Jesus married Mary Magdalene and had a child by her. This 'fact' apparently was hushed up by the early church, in particular the fourth-century emperor Constantine, who 'upgraded' Jesus to divine status, after three centuries where everyone considered him a mere mortal. In fact the book implies Jesus was really a devotee of the 'sacred feminine', the worship of nature and the goddess, yet all this was banned by the monolithic and repressive church.

Now Christians have understandably become hot under the collar about all this, arguing that it is a serious misrepresentation of their faith. As it happens, it's not too hard to show that this version of Christian origins is bizarre and should be taken with a very large bucket of salt. It has to be said that *The Da Vinci Code* is a great page-turner, pretty average literature and lousy history. The American magazine *Christianity Today* claims that the book has spawned at least nine refutations by Christian authors, showing how flawed it is historically and theologically. The problem is that although *The Da Vinci Code* has a staggering 17 million copies in print, the Christian refutations will struggle to sell 17,000. The problem is not their content – I'm sure all are better history than Dan Brown's book, and make a good case. The difficulty is the genre. Basically people read *The Da Vinci Code* not so much because of its ideas (after all, it is basically a book promoting old-style pre-Christian pagan goddess worship), but because it is such a great story. And how many books commending Christian faith do you know that come in the form of great stories? Well, there is one, of course – the Bible. It is fascinating that the central book of Christianity comes in the form not of a reasoned argument but a complex narrative, with as much suspense, surprise and intrigue, with as many devious villains and wonderful flawed heroes as any bestseller. And yet most books commending Christianity are cool, fairly academic works of mainly rational argument.

As the research presented here shows, the church faces a generation of people largely ignorant about some of the most basic features of Christian faith. The wider culture is awash with misunderstandings and misrepresentations, either deliberate or accidental. If Christians are to reverse this, then it will take far more than a few individual conversations or learned presentations in the form of standard academic argument.

Perhaps the reason why so many people turn away from the church is because its portrayal of God and of itself can so often

seem dull and uninteresting, compared with the stories told elsewhere. Earlier in the last century there were a number of Christian
authors who engaged in the writing of 'Christian' fiction of a more
or less explicit form, writers such as Dorothy L. Sayers, C. S. Lewis,
Charles Williams, G. K. Chesterton and, of course, J. R. R. Tolkien.
There are some novelists today who try to write with an implicit
Christian vision, but not many.[5] If Christian faith is to be taken more
seriously, it will take more than well-argued, worthy tomes of rationalist apologetics. It will need to engage the imagination with the
genres of literature and communication that are popular today –
especially novels, films, exhibitions, TV documentaries, newspapers
articles and the like. Probably the events that have generated most
public debate about Christian faith in recent years have been Mel
Gibson's film *The Passion of the Christ* and the National Gallery's exhi-
bition in 2000, *Seeing Salvation: The Image of Christ*. Neither of these was
a book. Neither was an official, church-sponsored event. Both had
massive coverage.

Early Christian apologists of the second century used the well-
known genre of the petition to the emperor as the initial form of
their writing, developing into more general writings in the style of
philosophical treatises like those written by their contemporaries in
Greek thought.[6] They chose the genres of literature best suited to
reach their world. It is odd, when you think of it, that we don't.

Perhaps the reason Christianity has been on the decline for
decades in the West is not so much that it was proved to be untrue,
but rather because it failed to appeal any more to the imagination. It
seemed dull, repressive, unexciting. It failed to capture the imagination of the culture as it did in the first few centuries of its history
when it really did appeal imaginatively to the Western world. In more
recent centuries, other stories appeared that held much more exciting promise for explaining the world, such as evolutionary biology,
sociology or psychology; or for changing it, such as Marxism or
(briefly) Fascism. It is unlikely that Christians will reverse the disdain
to their faith held by many without this kind of engagement with the
imagination. This kind of apologetics is very different from the kind
we are used to, but unless we Christians engage seriously in it, we are
likely to find ourselves more and more marginal to our culture.

There are a number of factors in church culture that militate against this kind of public engagement. One particular difficulty is a distinct bias in church culture away from the arts. Those of us who work in universities are often struck by the far greater preponderance of scientists who are Christians, than Christian academics or students studying arts subjects. Again, you hear of many Christians involved in sport but comparatively few engaged in drama, painting or literary criticism.

Perhaps because of ancient Protestant nervousness about images or a siege mentality when it comes to secular culture, many churches have little engagement with the arts, creative writing and the use of the image. When Christians do engage with artistic endeavour, it is often to complain about it. And yet we are a culture in love with and hugely influenced by images of every kind. Ideas, feelings and impressions are disseminated in our culture, not in scientific treatises or cold logical argumentation but by the careful crafting of language, the imagination of the advertising executive or the style of the designer.

The imagination is often distrusted in church culture, or at least less visual, more wordy forms of communication predominate, such as sermons, hymns or spoken liturgy on a page. Now, this is not to denigrate sermons. They remain one of the vital and central ways in which Christian faith is taught and passed on. Yet perhaps three-point, fifteen-minute sermons are more of a cultural construct than we think. Alongside them, and as part of them, what if churches consciously made an attempt to use more visual means of communication, encouraged church members with artistic gifts to use them creatively for God, and fostered the telling of honest tales about our own attempts to walk the Christian path? Then they might encourage more of a sense that it's not just OK to write stories, paint pictures with colours or words, design images that convey Christian truth, but it is essential if the kind of people discussed in these pages are to be touched. And that is simply because these are the very ways in which our culture disseminates its truth.

Prepared to be questioned

When asked what questions they would like to have answered, the people interviewed came up with responses we might have predicted: questions of destiny, purpose, creation, science, suffering, history and the spiritual realm. Yet another question also loomed large in the results of the research, as indicated in Chapter 1 – the difficulty people had with what they thought of as traditional pictures of God.

The idea of God as a positive, genial, spiritual force, always somewhat comforting, not exactly challenging, nor usually judgmental, was very common. As Chapter 1 clearly showed,[7] people found the idea of a personal God difficult – more abstract language sat more easily with most of them. The Christian image of God seemed to conjure up the traditional idea of an old man with a beard sitting on a cloud – an image people unsurprisingly felt they could not relate to. Prayer was valid only as a kind of psychological exercise, not because it received any answers or made a real difference.

What is interesting about this is, on the one hand, the surprising level of religious practice (a lot of people do actually pray in one way or another); and, on the other, the persistence of belief in God, albeit often a God far removed from Christian notions.

Some time ago I was sitting on a bus with a friend, a lapsed Catholic who was describing to me why he had drifted out of faith. There were several bad experiences of church in there somewhere, but the thing that stuck in my mind was that he found it hard to imagine God. Who or what is this 'God' that Christians talk about? If he isn't an old man with a beard on a cloud, then who is he? What does he look like, sound like, feel like? It was a question that stopped me in my tracks. How would I explain who God is to a frustrated enquirer like that?

Now, you can find answers to that question in other books – that isn't the purpose of this one. However, the point is that churches do need to help Christians think about these kinds of questions, partly so they know what they might say if such a question came up in conversation, but also because the same question may occur in their own mind, and stronger faith requires deeper understanding.

If Christians are to address the kinds of questions that will inevitably arise as soon as the conversation turns to God, then they will need to learn to be more articulate about their faith, and particularly about the common questions asked about it. And this will mean not just being prepared for the traditional problems like suffering, other faiths and the like, but also for less conventional ones like describing what God is like, or explaining why the *Da Vinci Code*'s history is flawed, or why Christianity appears less spiritual than its rivals. This doesn't mean feeding Christian people with easy, trite answers, but it does mean encouraging them to think about their faith. It will mean a steadily focused attention on encouraging lay Christians to take their faith seriously enough to test it out, to submit it to scrutiny, not being shielded from the harder questions. Too often a conspiracy of silence exists between clergy who think laity don't need to think too hard about the faith and can be fed brief, badly digested sermons, and laity who think of church as a haven from the world in which they can enjoy a respite from difficult questions.

Thinking through doubts, questions and difficulties in faith can be formative and constructive. It is also essential if the church (which of course means its millions of individual members in their conversations at work, home, the sports club or whatever) is to be able to dismantle the force field of regular objections to faith that keep many from belief.

Public apologists

One of the effects of the Enlightenment was effectively to privatize Christian faith into a personal opinion rather than a public truth. Hence the suspicion of many of the people interviewed about being told what to believe, or of the efforts of the evangelist. Religion is a private matter, so no-one is to intrude in that space in my life, any more than they are allowed to trespass into my garden without permission.

One knock-on effect of that has been to make Christians nervous of putting their heads above the parapet in public. Building local churches is fine. Concentrating on the local level is a fair strategy, but intruding with religion in the public sphere is rarely done, and you are likely to invite a fair degree of opprobrium if you do.

It is hard to name the top-class Christian apologists of today. It's easier to name top theologians, Christians prominent in business, politics or science (less so in the arts, sadly), even some big-name evangelists. But try to name pre-eminent apologists, especially in the UK, and the names are harder to find.[8] Most prominent Christian writers, the top five Christian authors to come to mind, are mostly known for their writing for other Christians. Theologians or writers who can interpret the Christian faith for a non-Christian world with wit and clarity are few and far between.

There is an urgent need for such people. In Oxford, a new 'Centre for Evangelism and Apologetics' has been launched as part of Wycliffe Hall, aiming to train people for such a ministry, but despite such ventures there is still some way to go before we have the kinds of people who can write intelligently, entertainingly and persuasively about Christian faith in newspapers and magazines, not to mention the kinds of fiction and TV media that are the primary means of influencing minds and hearts in our culture. Serious attention needs to be given to identify, develop and encourage such people in this vital role.

A different audience

Earlier in this chapter we noted the early Christian predilection for apologetics, especially in the second century, and the fading of its use in subsequent years when Christianity gradually moved into the dominant position at the centre of the Graeco-Roman empire and culture. In the second century, theology was done mainly with an eye to the common criticisms of the faith regularly voiced by the church's contemporaries. So, for example, one common criticism was that Christianity was novel, a ridiculous story of a god who had just appeared out of nowhere on earth in human form a couple of hundred years before – a story that lacked the antiquity and venerable age of the myths of the old Greek gods, or pagan practices.

Justin Martyr, a Christian apologist, developed a sophisticated yet simple way of combating this. He borrowed an idea common in contemporary Stoic philosophy, which had also been used in the prologue to John's Gospel. This was the notion that God created the world though his 'Word' (*logos* in Greek), that this *logos* now permeates the world, and can be found in all that is good, true and wise. Justin's stroke of brilliance was to suggest that it was this *logos* that became incarnate in Jesus of Nazareth. Therefore Justin could argue that the coming of Jesus was not some event out of the blue, but was in fact the culmination of all creation – the entry into the world of the One through whom it had been created. Other philosophers and wise men had glimpsed snatches of this *logos* in their philosophies, but now the *logos* had come in its fullness in Jesus, and should be acknowledged and worshipped by all who love the truth. It was a way of helping Greeks who understood the idea of *logos* but could not make any sense of Jesus or the Jewish idea of the Messiah to begin to understand what Christians were talking about – helping them grasp Christian faith in a way that made sense to them.

This was a risky path. In fact in later years, this idea of the *logos*, taken in careless directions, led to some problems in Christian theology. However, the point is not so much the content of the idea but the method. Here was Christian theology done not in its own little world, oblivious of whether or not it made sense to anyone on the fringes of faith. Instead, it tried to remain true to its own identity, be thoroughly biblical and distinctively Christian, yet also remain conscious of the need to make some sense to those who didn't yet believe it.

This applies in a whole variety of areas of church life today. It applies to the writing of Christian theology, to the preaching of sermons, and the language of Christian conversation. And this is a hard path to tread. It is much easier either to retreat into a Christian bubble where we make sense to each other in our own private language, but are unfathomable to anyone outside that; or, on the other hand, to be so keen to relate to the world around that we translate Christian faith into forms and practices that end up losing Christian identity and distinctives altogether.

It is a good test, not just of evangelistic sermons but of any sermon, to ask, 'If someone wandered in from the street this morning, would they be able to make any sense of what is being said?' Would it speak into their lives, or make any discernible difference if they listened seriously?

The point is that theology in a secular culture (and by 'theology' is meant not just books, but ordinary sermons, Bible studies; in fact, any 'talk about God', which is what 'theo-logy' means) needs to be done with an eye to the audience outside the church as well as within it. That is not to say that central Christian belief is watered down or weakened in any way – far from it. It is simply to say that the way we express Christian truth needs to be always intelligible to those who stand on the fringes of belief, and who know next to nothing about it. It also means that some form of training in the kind of apologetics we have outlined here needs to become an essential part of training for the clergy and church leaders of the future.

Chapters 1 and 3 pointed to high levels of ignorance about

Christian doctrine, a desire to believe among many people and hesitancy about how well founded unbelief was. The very tentative, shallow nature of disbelief today, and the wistfulness with which it is often mixed, demand a more humble, modest and gentle apologetics than was demanded in more rigorously rationalistic days. Apologetics must learn this different style – gently suggesting, offering inducements and being sensitive to the genres in which ideas are circulated today – if it is to convince those who would like to believe but cannot.

Notes to Chapter 4

1. See http://www.churchsurvey.co.uk.
2. See Graham Tomlin, *The Provocative Church* (SPCK, 2002).
3. John Stackhouse, *Humble Apologetics: Defending the Faith Today* (OUP, 2002), pp. 119–120.
4. Ibid., p. 113.
5. Examples would include Susan Howatch, G. P. Taylor's *Shadowmancer* series, some of the work of Piers Paul Read and, in the USA, the excellent Pulitzer-prize-winning author Marilynne Robinson. Of course, the *Left Behind* series by Tim LaHaye and Jerry Jenkins is phenomenally successful in the USA, yet has made, and is likely to make, little impact in the UK, perhaps because of its controversial apocalyptic theology.
6. Robert M. Grant, *Greek Apologists of the Second Century* (Westminster, 1988), ch. 1.
7. Although this section responds to material laid out in Chapter 1 of this book, it clearly has implications for apologetics as well as spirituality, so it is dealt with here as well.
8. There are some: Alister McGrath has recently started to write for a wider audience in his two critical analyses of atheists and atheism: Alister E. McGrath, *Dawkins' God* (Blackwell, 2004); Alister E. McGrath, *The Twilight of Atheism: The Rise and Fall of Disbelief in the Modern World* (Doubleday, 2004). David Cook appeared for many years on *The Moral Maze*, and in the USA and elsewhere, Ravi Zacharias is notable for his work in this area. Jonathan Sacks is an excellent example of a rabbi who brilliantly explains the Jewish perspective to a secular audience.

SECTION 3 | **CHRISTIANS**

There are two types of 'Christian' in Britain today: the 'unofficial' type, for whom the word denotes little more than 'decent, British and spiritually minded', and the 'official' type, who attends church, likes to sing hymns but is commonly criticized for being hypocritical and intolerant. Neither is particularly close to the New Testament's idea of a Christian. The church needs to recapture the meaning of the word 'Christian', by developing a stronger sense of Christian identity, a more visible presence in society and a commitment to public action that expresses the goodness of God.

5. 'UN/OFFICIAL' CHRISTIANS

The results of the 2001 National Census came as something of a disappointment to secularists. Years of falling church attendance figures had prepared them for a decidedly irreligious response to the controversial faith group question. The results, when eventually published in early 2003, revealed nothing of the kind. Instead, they showed that 71% of people in England and Wales, 67% of people in Scotland and (less surprisingly) 86% of people in Northern Ireland claimed to belong to a religious group.[1] Despite the fact that the question was the only voluntary one asked, only 7% of people declined to give an answer and 15% said they had no religion. There was no social pressure on people to call themselves Christian in the way there might have been had the question been asked in 1951, and in any case such social pressure was unlikely to have been felt in people's own homes where the Census questionnaires were completed. Everyone knew that 'hardly anyone' went to church anymore, so why did 40-odd million people willingly tick 'Christian' when asked which religious group they belonged to?

For those acquainted with recent social research surveys, the result was less surprising. According to the Office for National Statistics' 1999 Social Trends Survey, around half of all adult British men and two-thirds of women regarded themselves as belonging to a religion.[2] The polling company MORI asked people their religious denomination throughout the 1990s and reported that 87% claimed to have a religion in 1992 and 78% in 2001.[3]

The common criticism levelled at these figures – that they are 'nominal' – entirely misses the point. Declaring your religious group is, by definition, a nominal activity: it is about which name you wish to associate yourself with in a public context. Asking people which religious group they belong to says nothing about either what they believe or what they do about it. It is a question of whom they wish to be associated with, of what badge they want to wear.

The real issue, however, is not that an obstinately large number of people still want to associate themselves with the label 'Christian', nor how 'nominal' that self-association is, but what precisely is understood by that word itself. What actually *is* a Christian?

'Words', T. S. Eliot once wrote, 'decay with imprecision.' They 'will not stay in place, will not stay still'. The more abstract, socially mediated and popularly used a word is, the more this is the case, as can be seen all too clearly in the way the word 'Christian' is used. Much like its monumental counterpart, Westminster Abbey, years of standing at the centre of British life, with all the traffic of nationhood passing by and through it, have seen layers of meaning accrete on its face. What might once have been a reasonably clean and clear façade (although it is doubtful whether the word 'Christian' was ever free of social connotations, even when it was first used in Antioch in the AD 40s) has been covered in a film of contemporary concerns and values, to the extent that today the word does not mean what the dictionaries tell us it means. A Christian may be officially defined as 'one who professes belief in Jesus as Christ or follows the religion based on the life and teachings of Jesus', but that is not what many of the 37 million people in England and Wales had in mind when they ticked 'Christian' on the 2001 Census form.

The research for this book showed that the word 'Christian' has a spectrum of meanings, with the 'unofficial' Christian standing at one end and the 'official' one at the other.

'Unofficial' Christians

The 'unofficial' definition of 'Christian' had two elements to it.

Firstly, it meant 'good'. An 'unofficial' Christian was a good person. Interviewees repeatedly confirmed this fact, with statements such as 'kindness is the bottom line in Christians' or '[a Christian is] a warm, caring, happy, sympathetic person' or 'a balanced human being'. Inevitably, interviewees recognized that this was the ideal rather than the reality and that few 'Christians' actually lived up to it, but, crucially, these definitions indicated what it was that they were aspiring to when they called themselves 'Christian'.

One of the commonest definitions of the goodness that lay at the heart of being a Christian was that it entailed listening without judging. One elderly woman said that '[a Christian is] helpful, open and honest . . . [and] needs to be able to listen and not judge', and in doing so highlighted a tension that a number of interviewees recognized. Just as 'Christian' is a socially mediated, abstract noun, susceptible to 'decay [and] imprecision', so is the word 'good'. Whereas in 1500 the word 'good' would have meant something like 'pious' or 'loyal', and in 1900 it would have meant 'honourable', in early twenty-first-century Britain it means 'tolerant'. Being a *real* Christian means 'being tolerant of everybody else' or 'non-judgmental' – an association that, as we shall see below, left some interviewees with a rather confusing contradiction to explain.

The second, more subtle element within the definition of the 'unofficial' Christian linked the word to a sense of nationhood.[4] No interviewee ever asserted outright that one had to be Christian, still less Anglican, to be English and, indeed, few made any explicit connection between religion and nationality. As the ICM survey for 'What the world thinks about God' suggested, people in the UK are highly conscious of the dangers of linking religious affiliation with national identity.

Nevertheless, people's attitudes were occasionally revealed, almost by accident, in what they said. One middle-aged man, when talking, extremely uncertainly, about Islam, about which he admitted knowing very little, inadvertently advertised his affiliation in his casual use of the first person plural (emphasis mine):

> Jesus or whatever name . . . other religions use the same sort of person. I mean, the Muslims have got Mohammed, haven't they? It is very similar to *ours*.

In a similar, if slightly bizarre example, one young man who, by his own admission, had no interest in or sympathy with the Christian faith, made a curiously aggressive attack on the commercialism of Christianity, in which he said:

> You don't see shops advertising, 'Come and get a Ramadan offer.' It just . . . it's a bit out of order really. I'm not, like, well into my religion but from my point of view it is abuse really.

'Unofficial' Christian was, therefore, a label that people wore in as far as they felt it proclaimed their own sense of moral goodness (which, in the current climate, largely means tolerance) and, in a more understated way, their own sense of belonging. 'I am' (or, more self-effacingly) 'I like to consider myself Christian' meant 'I like to think I am a good, decent, tolerant person, whose roots are in English culture and society.'

'Official' Christians

The 'official' Christian was rather different. First and foremost, he or she was part of 'official' Christianity, and 'official' Christianity is a 'religion'. 'Religion', rather like the word 'Christian', only more so, has changed meaning over time, becoming an almost irretrievably dirty word in the process. Brief word-association exercises during some of the interviews conducted for this book showed how deep was the condemnation that the word 'religion' had attracted. People automatically associated it with words like 'stuffy, discipline, brainwashing, hypocrites, conflict, war, corruption, differences, [and] devastation'. In contrast, there was not a single association that could be understood as in any way positive.

The length to which some people were prepared to go to dissociate themselves from the word, in spite of their own beliefs and behaviour, was, on occasion, almost comical. In one interview, we asked an elderly widow whether she believed in God. 'Yes, absolutely,' she replied. 'Do you think you can communicate with this God?' we went on. 'Yes, I think it is necessary to pray,' she replied, continuing, 'I wouldn't describe myself as a religious person but I certainly believe in God and I certainly believe in the power of prayer.' In spite of her theistic beliefs and practice, she was prepared to do almost anything to dissociate herself from the label 'religious'.

'Religion' is itself, of course, very difficult to define and almost uselessly vague as a term, but that exacerbated rather than addressed the problem. The local parish church and al-Qaeda are both 'religious', and even though not even the most hostile interviewee claimed that the local vicar was a malign influence on society, that made little difference. Guilt was by association, and the 'official' Christian was, for circumstances entirely out of his or her control, tarred with the loathsome brush of 'religion'.

Beyond this guilt by association, the 'official' Christian was recognized and defined primarily by what he or she did or said, rather than by what they believed. This incorporated a range of factors, such as church-going, proclaiming an objective moral code, being 'born again', a Bible-basher or pious, all of which were largely alien to the life of the 'unofficial' Christian.

There was often a shadow of disapproval that hung over these factors and, on occasion, such 'official' Christians were subject to some extraordinarily nasty criticism, being labelled 'patronizing, desperate for support, colourless, begging for money, misfits, goody two-shoes, [and] holier than thou'.

Such abuse was almost invariably levelled at the *abstract* Christian, however, and was rarely supported by actual, personal encounters. 'Christians' as a *type* may be unpleasant but my colleague at work or my next-door neighbour, who has a name and a face, was often altogether different. Hence, when one interviewee suddenly recollected that his neighbours were 'religious', there was a tone of genuine surprise in his voice (note the telling 'But' in line 2):

> We've got neighbours like that. I don't know what religion they follow, but they live for it, and the children, literally . . . But they are cracking people . . . they are really, really nice people and, actually, thinking back when she had a baby recently, the gifts and the food, you know, visitors they had, unbelievable. Unbelievable, they were queuing at the door.

Not only did a number of interviewees know such 'official' Christians, but some had even benefited from their love and concern.

One man, in his early forties, whose wife had recently died of cancer, leaving him to bring up their infant daughter, told a particularly moving story of how local Christians had helped him out. It is worth repeating in full:

> I got a huge amount of support from the church, because my wife was ill . . . she was quite Catholic, and she got a huge amount of support from the local Baptist church . . . she was ill for about two or three years, and when she died my daughter and I, we got a lot of support from them. It was just the support that I needed from fellow human beings. After the event, and continuing support. And a real community spirit, you know, inviting us to their houses, bringing food to my house . . . it was totally genuine. When it's from the heart there's a difference. They didn't expect me to actually go to church, although I felt as though I should have gone and continued to go, but my beliefs had changed and I don't think they frowned upon that, you know. I could have continued, I could have perhaps converted in some way, but I didn't.

His powerful story was both depressing, for the trauma he and his daughter had experienced, and encouraging, for the example set by the Christians from his local Baptist church (of which he had never been a member) who had reached out to him so genuinely.

It was also depressing, however, that experiences like this, and encounters like the one mentioned previously, did little to change the overall attitude towards 'official' Christians. This individual was, not surprisingly, less inclined to condemn 'official' Christians than other people interviewed, and his experience was perhaps the most positive mentioned. But sadly, in spite of other genuinely positive encounters with 'official' Christians in many walks of life, the overall impression was still negative and the attitude still hostile. It was as if the pleasing odour given off by such encounters was not enough to change the lingering (and less traceable) anti-'official'-Christian stench that pervaded the atmosphere.

Tension and clarity
These two images, of the 'unofficial' and 'official' Christian, co-existed in many people's minds, occasionally causing them some

tension. Interviewees did not, of course, use the terms 'unofficial' or 'official', instead employing only the word 'Christian' in such a way as sometimes confused their explanations. On several occasions, they felt the need to distinguish between the types of Christian they were discussing, by resorting to further labels and clarifications.

One middle-aged man said, of 'official' Christians, 'They like to think of themselves as being kind of Christian but in my understanding of the word they are not.' He continued, 'It's a kind of paradox . . . [they say] they are Christian and . . . superficially they do all the things that Christians should do but in terms of the way they treat others and behave . . . that actually is not very Christian.'

A young woman, in a telling comment, said, 'The people I know are non-conventional Christians. They are so lovely, so warm, not Bible-bashers. They are not do-gooders, they are just lovely, lovely people.' For her, these Christians were likeable *despite* being 'officially' (i.e. 'Bible-bashing') Christian.

She went on to explain what exactly she meant by saying, 'A stereotypical Christian is someone who is against sin. Very straight-laced, conformist, very narrow-minded to a degree about what is right and what is wrong.' Having said that, she also recognized that the Christians she knew did all the things that 'official' Christians were supposed to do (attend church, pray, sing etc.) and that there was therefore something wrong in this simple distinction she had drawn between, in her words, 'conventional' and 'non-conventional' Christians. Thus she conceded that the 'stereotypical Christian' about whom she had been talking was probably more of a myth than a reality, reasoning, 'I don't think that is the reality of it at all but that is how the press portrays them.'

Such an admission was unusual, with more people assuming that the 'official'-Christian stereotype was the more accurate one and that their positive encounters with such Christians were the exceptions.

That said, this tension disappeared and the difference between 'official' and 'unofficial' Christians became clear when interviewees talked about two issues that vexed them as much as any others: tolerance and hypocrisy. Tolerance was, as noted in Chapter 3, the supreme value in the moral universe of most people. It was, in the mind of many interviewees, *the* panacea for the world's ills. Its veneration was, on occasion, so extreme that it even resulted in a rather ironic form of quasi-fascism or 'totalitolerance', in which those groups judged to be intolerant were themselves deemed intolerable. In order for tolerance to maintain itself, it needed to be intolerant.

Despite this logical flaw, it was over the issue of tolerance that the difference between 'official' and 'unofficial' Christians was seen most clearly. It was not that 'official' Christians were intolerant whereas 'unofficial' Christians, like many of the interviewees themselves, were not. 'Unofficial' Christians could also express intolerance (although they tended not to call it that) and they often did, usually about the supposed policies of local councils towards ethnic minorities.

It was more that 'official' Christians were intolerant of the *wrong* things or, alternatively, of *too many* things. The common objection that 'Christians are intolerant' was, in essence, shorthand for 'Christians are intolerant of things that I am not intolerant of,' usually things to do with sexual practice, family set-ups or some other exercise of personal freedom.

It is worth noting, if only in passing, that a large number of interviewees (indeed, for all intents and purposes, all of them) registered serious concerns about the state of British society, citing family breakdown, lack of discipline and respect, instant-gratification omni-consumerism, and 'value-less' TV (by which they meant wrong-value TV) among the reasons. At the root of many of these problems was the concern that we were a selfish and overly permissive society – one, in other words, that was not intolerant enough. Although it was never drawn, there was an obvious link here to the intolerance criticisms levelled at 'official' Christians.

The second issue over which the distinction between 'official' and 'unofficial' Christians was clearest was that of hypocrisy. Hypocrisy was the single most frequently mentioned term in word-association exercises. Along with being intolerant, the 'official' Christian was almost universally charged with hypocrisy. The interesting thing about this charge, however, was that it was something of a self-fulfilling prophecy. Those interviewees who talked about their own moral codes, often took considerable pride in them, and vigorously defended the idea that you could be moral without being 'Christian'. To suggest otherwise was to offer real offence. 'I've got high morals but I would never say I was religious,' one young woman said. 'I'd never do anything to hurt anybody or . . . whereas sometimes if you meet some people who are very religious, they sort of shove it down your throat.'

The crucial factor in such explanations was that no matter how elevated these self-professed moral standards were, they were invariably *self-designated*. Without exception, all respondents who professed a moral code were very clear that it was *their* moral code. Indeed, they took real pride is explaining that they did not broadcast their morality but rather went about it silently. 'I don't have to go round pretending that I am going to be holy,' one middle-aged woman explained, '[just] as long as I'm good and kind to people, and basically look after [and] be good to my family.'

The idea of adhering to someone else's moral code was anathema. Indeed, it was precisely the autonomy of having one's own moral code that marked interviewees off, in their own minds at least, as adults. It was a key part of the freedom, independence and scepticism that showed them to be intelligent, modern people, and stood them in direct contrast to 'official Christians'.

'If you were church[-going],' one middle-aged woman reasoned, 'you are going to live by the church's morals, where they tell you what to do rather than [have you] thinking for yourself what is good and bad, and making your own opinion.' In contrast to this, 'My choice is that the church doesn't come into it, and I just live my life as I believe I should live it, and make my decisions and hope they are good ones.'

This sounds like a wholly reasonable and mature approach to ethical living, but it has the side-effect of indemnifying people against the charge of hypocrisy. This is because, if you do not pronounce an objective and observable moral code, you cannot be accused of failing it. Declaring that you have your own personal, powerful moral compass is not only admirable but is safe, as it effectively means that no-one can tell how far short of it you might fall. If hypocrisy is not walking the talk, when no-one knows what your talk is, no-one can accuse you of not walking it. The result is a self-fulfilling prophecy: only those brave or stupid enough to admit to following an objective and observable moral code, which usually means Christians or perhaps 'religious people', can be accused of not walking the talk. Only such people *can* be hypocrites.

Very occasionally, this fact was revealed in an interview. During one group session, a number of interviewees forcefully declared their hatred of hypocrisy and of the (religious) people they thought were hypocrites. They then went on to talk about the fatuousness of Christian belief and also the way in which the church did little for society as a whole. When, later in the interview, several respondents revealed that they were godparents themselves, or that they had had their own children baptized, or that they had found ways and means of getting their children into the local church school, they were forced to admit their own hypocrisy, albeit in a tongue-in-cheek way.

'We are saying they are hypocrites, but we are also hypocrites,' one woman admitted. 'I mean, I've got a lot of godchildren that my friends have had christened,' she continued, 'so in a way that's hypocritical isn't it?' Another interviewee responded, 'That is what happened when I had my three children christened . . . hypocritical really isn't it . . . I had to go to church for about x amount of weeks.'

For once, because of the wide-ranging nature of the interview, these individuals had had their self-indemnifying position exposed. Their tactics – which amounted to a kind of guerrilla morality, in which they used their nimble, personalized and well-concealed moral outlooks to attack Christians, whose own moral standards were well known, publicly visible and, therefore, fatefully exposed – had caught up with them.

None of this is to suggest, of course, that 'official' Christians cannot be either offensively intolerant or distastefully hypocritical. 'Official' and 'unofficial' Christians alike know that to be the case. It is to underline, however, that the yawning gap between these two types of Christian – the gap through which any biblically rooted concept of what a Christian really is (or should be) had fallen – is, to some extent, self-fulfilling.

The end result is that the word 'Christian' is dirtied and corrupted to the point of redundancy. When 40 million people call themselves Christian in the National Census, yet use the label to mean 'good and/or British' and know or care little about Jesus Christ, the word is drained of much of its colour. When any supposedly Christ-loving Christians act in unpleasantly aggressive, intolerant or hypocritical ways, and then have their behaviour broadcast to millions, the word is further damaged. When the social and cultural air we breathe exacerbates those charges of intolerance and hypocrisy, so that

Christians become hypocritical or intolerant almost by definition, the word is still further mutilated.

No bad-smelling words are beyond redemption. 'Tory', 'Whig' and 'Prime Minister', for example, each started life as a term of abuse. The task before Christians in Britain today is to rescue the word 'Christian'.

Notes to Chapter 5

1. See www.statistics.gov.uk.
2. Office for National Statistics, *Social Trends 1999*.
3. See www.mori.com.
4. All interviews, it should be noted, were conducted in England. Responses would, in this respect, be different in Scotland, Wales or Northern Ireland.

6. AUTHENTIC CHRISTIANS

Chapter 5 can be summed up in a single and simple statement: 'official' Christianity has an image problem. And that is a *big* problem in a world where the image is king. The all-pervasive and hugely influential media of TV, newspapers, websites and magazines shape the way we think in ways we barely notice, let alone understand. In those media, in the forms of interaction that control opinions and direct our unconscious reactions, the general image that comes across about 'official' Christianity is largely a negative one. Yes, there are occasional positive images of Christianity and Christians, yet so often the 'religion' stories in the media revolve around Christians arguing over property, doctrine or sex, or scandals involving paedophile priests or money-grabbing evangelists.

But does it really matter? Perhaps Christians shouldn't play the image game at all. Does it really matter what the TV producers think – isn't it more important what God thinks? Maybe Christians have to expect a bad reputation. Pehaps persecution and misunderstanding are part of the territory for any faithful church or Christian?

Well, yes, to an extent, all that must be right. However, despite expecting the inevitability of some kind of misunderstanding and persecution, the New Testament writers do show quite some concern for the way in which Christians are viewed from the outside. It is important that Christian leaders 'have a good reputation with outsiders' (1 Timothy 3:7). Christians are to do what they can to ensure a good reputation in the wider society: 'Do not repay anyone evil for evil. Be careful to do what is right in the eyes of everybody. If it is possible, as far as it depends on you, live at peace with everyone' (Romans 12:17–18). The key note here is 'as far as it depends on you' – if Christians are criticized in the press unfairly, so be it. Yet they should still do what they can to win a good reputation among their peers.

Yet it often seems that this is a losing battle. Christians often complain that the media are unfair to their faith. They often grumble that journalists will pick up on bad news stories, not positive ones – good news is no news. Yet such complaints do not really solve the problem. Newspaper articles will pick up on anything out of the ordinary, whether positive or negative – the question is whether there really are many genuinely interesting, good news stories around about the church. The debate about whether the media creates or reflects the nature of society remains a hot issue, and the reason why it is hot is surely that it does both. Comment on what happens in the church – which, after all, is a public body in an open society – is inevitable. Christians might with some justification grumble about the portrayal of the faith in public media, but the onus is upon Christians themselves to make news by ensuring that, slowly but surely, the image of 'church' changes over the coming years and decades. As Mark Thompson, Director General of the BBC, himself a committed Christian, puts it: 'we have plenty more to do to reflect religion positively on our airwaves – particularly Christianity, where despite some real advances in recent years, there is still something of a creative deficit'.[1]

Perhaps that very 'creative deficit' reflects the poverty of Christian life in Britain, one of the most secularized countries in the world. The insight highlighted by Chapter 5 – that the single most common word associated with 'Christian' is 'hypocrite' – is as embarrassing as it is surprising. Christians may feel with some justification that it is unfair, and a good answer to the common jibe that the church is full of hypocrites might be the old line 'Well, that doesn't matter. Come and join us – one more won't make any difference!'

However, when criticized, it is always wise practice to ask what lies behind the criticism. Is there any germ of truth in it, however unfair or hurtful? It may be that the uncomfortable truth behind this revealing finding is that Christians claim a lot but don't deliver much. Behind all the words, the theology, the sermons and the books, people don't really see much noticeable difference between the way of life of the average Christian and that of the average non-Christian. And that is made worse by the sense that Christians have a lot to say about what a difference Christianity makes.

Image change

Other groups in society have affected such change over time. Whatever we make of the church debates over homosexuality, the change in public perception of homosexuals and the homosexual community over the past decade or so is remarkable. Twenty years ago, derogatory language or sniggering comments about homosexuals were common even in public settings. There was still much public suspicion of gay people, jokes in TV sitcoms, and a general mood of opinion that homosexual behaviour was ridiculous, seditious, unacceptable and to be frowned upon. Of course, not all that has disappeared, nor have the debates entirely gone away, yet the public attitude to homosexuality has altered significantly, leading towards a very different approach. The campaign for gay rights has been remarkably successful, so that now even questioning the legitimacy of a gay lifestyle is likely to be denounced as homophobia. The public image of gay people is also much more likely to be positive too – emphasizing creativity or sensitivity rather than effeminacy or deviousness.

The point is simply that such image change is possible for groups who are determined to create a different view of themselves in the public arena. Maybe something like this has to happen for the Christian church too. But can the church change its image? And if so, how might it do this in a way that is authentically Christian, rather than just clever or fundamentally secular?

It might be thought that the best way to approach this issue would be to hire the best media consultants to mount a vigorous advertising campaign to change the public perception of Christianity. After all, that is what a business would do. It would also look into the possibility of rebranding. Anderson Consulting changed its name to

'Accenture', British Steel joined with a Dutch Company to became 'Corus' and the good old Post Office became 'Consignia' for a few years, and then changed back, as no-one knew what the new name meant. Maybe the church needs a new name, to disassociate itself from a murky past. Is the answer to be found in rebranding or the appointment of market researchers as bishops?

A Christian strategy for image change

As it happens, the New Testament has a very clear strategy on what to do when the church is maligned or has a bad image. It is not to mount an aggressive media campaign, with 'instant rebuttal' mechanisms to spring into action whenever a vicar is accused of running off with the organist. Nor is it to employ dozens of market analysts to discern what people want and give it to them. Closer to home, it is not even to mount a vigorous evangelistic campaign in every city of the land with a world-renowned speaker, nor even to mobilize an army of Christian journalists to write church-friendly articles in the public press.

The strategy is as simple as it is clear. Put most simply, in the words of Jesus himself, it is this: 'Let your light shine before men, that they may see your good deeds and praise your Father in heaven' (Matthew 5:16). The same note is struck again and again throughout these pages. Faced by critics who want to carp and criticize? Don't argue back, just act: 'for it is God's will that by doing good you should silence the ignorant talk of foolish men' (1 Peter 2:15). And then again, Peter's advice for Christians living in a world where they are more likely to get misrepresented and suffer unjust accusations is to 'live such good lives among the pagans that, though they accuse you of doing wrong, they may see your good deeds and glorify God on the day he visits us'.[2]

The common thread to all these passages is simple: Doing good. The truly Christian way of winning a good reputation for the gospel is for the local church to begin thinking seriously about what practical good can be done in its local community, planning carefully with the resources it has, putting a strategy together and getting on with it.

What this means theologically is that the true location of Christian behaviour is not in the doctrine of salvation but in the doctrine of mission. Often in the past, the motivation for acts of Christian goodness, generosity, kindness and the like was that in some way they contributed to the individual's salvation, either as acquiring merit (the Catholic version), or confirming one's calling and election (the Calvinist version). The way Jesus and Peter put it suggests that the reason Christians are to give themselves to practical action, acts of goodness and kindness to both friends and enemies, is at least in part to make the kingdom of God visible, to point and bear witness to it, to make outsiders sit up and take notice, and to lead them to glorify God.

Protestants rightly rejected the idea that good deeds were the grounds of salvation, insisting that God's love and forgiveness do not depend on our first doing good things for God, but instead on trust in the merits of Christ. But they then struggled to work out why we should still do good, if in fact we are saved by faith, not works. Perhaps the reason is that they failed to locate Christian behaviour in the right place theologically. It became either a proof of predestination, or a simple expression of gratitude. (Which is all very well, but the implication is that it still remains optional – if I receive a present from my aunt and forget to write the thank-you letter, I still keep the present. The letter is nice but not much really hangs on it.) On the other hand, if practical Christian goodness is a necessity for the sake of mission, so that through the transformation of people and communities, others might see, wonder and believe, then it gathers an urgency and centrality in the life of the church that it so often lacks.

The New Testament emphasis falls repeatedly not on words, arguments or clever media manipulation, but instead on gaining a well-deserved reputation for doing good. The idea is to change the public perception so that when the word 'Christian' is mentioned, the image it conjures up is not so much 'hypocrisy' but 'goodness', 'compassion' or 'generosity'.

Aristides was an Athenian philosopher who became a Christian around the middle of the second century. He later wrote a piece praising the Christians to their pagan neighbours, perhaps reflecting something of what drew him to this new faith.

> They do not commit adultery or fornication, nor do they bear false witness, nor covet the things of others; they honour father and mother

and love their neighbours; they give right judgement and they never do to others what they would not wish to happen to themselves. They comfort those that wrong them and make friends of them. They are eager to do good to their enemies. They are meek and gentle . . . They do not despise the widow and do not oppress the orphan. He that has gives ungrudgingly to him that has not. If they see a stranger they take him under their roof and rejoice over him, as if he were their own brother. They are ready to lay down their own lives for the sake of Christ.[3]

Maybe it is an idealized picture and a bit exaggerated, but try to imagine a twenty-first-century intellectual converted to Christianity writing something similar today. Perhaps if this was closer to the general reputation Christians had today, we might see church growth in the twenty-first century as rapid as in the first and second. If this is the kind of public perception of Christianity to which the church today might aspire, then the way is clear – it is by focusing on an agenda of 'doing good'.

The common perception outlined in Chapter 5 that a Christian was basically a 'good person' has some theological flaws, but in some sense it is not a bad instinct. It is what people expect from Christians, and perhaps have a right to expect. By the self-designation of 'Christian', it seems that many people simply mean they consider themselves not to be a bad person – if I don't steal, murder, cheat and lie, then I am kind of 'Christian'. However, real Christianity is not just an absence of badness. It involves positive goodness. And a church which displays that in a whole host of simple, practical ways, which offers the chance for ordinary people to get involved in relieving poverty, suffering and pain, will begin to show up conventional 'goodness' (i.e. not having done bad things) for what it is – a pale imitation of the real thing, a shadow of the reality.

Of course, all this sounds far too simple to make a difference, and it's far harder to work out what that means in practice than to issue high-sounding appeals to action. But if this is a clear New Testament emphasis, then it needs to be taken seriously. The rest of this chapter outlines ways in which this agenda might be carried out.

Christian identity

A change to the public perception of the word 'Christian' requires a much stronger sense of Christian identity than we are used to. What we want others to know about us says a lot about who we think we are. If someone lets you know fairly soon after you have met them that they support Manchester United, are Irish, or have three children, that will tell you quite a lot about what really matters to them, about their identity. To be too eager to tell everybody about these things betrays a measure of insecurity, but being happy to be known as a Man United supporter/Irish/proud mother simply states something powerful about what lies closest to our hearts.

For the vast majority of the 70% who ticked the box 'Christian' in the National Census, their allegiance was to a kind of 'Christianity-lite', a vague notion of belonging to the Christian religion rather than anything else, an 'unofficial Christianity' that seemed to mean little more than what you wanted it to mean. It meant a self-designation as a 'good person'. Most likely it was fairly far down the list of words that people would use to describe themselves – or at least it seemed to be for most of the interviewees questioned for this book. Yet for the church to change its public image will mean individual Christians coming to understand that allegiance to Christ means more than buying another brand. I may be a Man United supporter, Irish or a proud father, but if I am a Christian, then those things can never be my core identity – that belongs solely to Christ. This is what Paul means when he writes that 'there is neither Jew nor Greek, slave nor free, for you are all one in Christ Jesus' (Galatians 3:28). The whole argument of the letter focuses upon the point that the central identity of the Christian is no longer derived from ethnicity, gender, employment, family or anything else. Instead, we are given a new identity in baptism and conversion – 'I have been crucified with Christ and I no longer live, but Christ lives in me' (Galatians 2:20).

This point about Christian identity was so important for Paul that he confronted Peter to his face and was prepared to scupper his career over it.[4] It was for Paul not a peripheral, vaguely interesting bit of Christian theology. It was central to the gospel. Christ's death and resurrection had brought about a new order, where the old divisions of Jew/Gentile, slave/free, male/female were not done away with but made secondary and provisional in the light of the new creation of people in Christ.

It is this kind of teaching that is vital in our setting. Only a strong sense of Christian identity – that I am Christian before I am anything else – can sustain Christian witness in a competitive, brand- and image-conscious marketplace. Of course, it is possible to use the badge of 'Christian' as a means of causing further division, as happened in Lebanon, for example, in the 1970s and 1980s where 'Christian militia' fought against Muslim groups for power, or in Northern Ireland, where 'Protestant' or 'Catholic' became labels for communities in conflict. That kind of Christian identity makes the word 'Christian' yet another tribal grouping, another form of ethnicity, which is far from the kind of Christian identity that Paul has in mind. For him, being 'in Christ' means becoming part of the community through which God wishes to bless the world. It means a commitment to Christ's way of love, and a calling to give oneself for others as he did, to be the servant and not the master. A call for a stronger sense of Christian identity is not a call for militancy or strident, shrill activism. It is instead a call to be conformed to Christ, to speak his name, to act in that name, and to be prepared to do that publicly.

Lesslie Newbigin argued that 'missions are the test of our faith that the gospel is true'.[5] The gospel cannot prove its truth by recourse to some higher court of appeal; after all, there is no higher court of appeal than God himself. Yet, if that is the case, Christian faith is open to the charge that it is purely self-referential and subjective, a circular argument – it is true because it is true. How is this dilemma resolved? Following Michael Polanyi, Newbigin says:

> while we hold our beliefs as personally committed subjects, we hold them with universal intent, and we express that intent by publishing them and inviting all people to consider and accept them. To be willing so to publish them is the test of our real belief. In this sense missions are the test of our faith.[6]

The willingness to let our Christian faith and identity be known, whether by silent signs, words or actions performed in the name of Christ, is the true test of whether we really believe the gospel to be ultimately true, not just a private choice, like going to the gym or a secret belief in fairies. I could simply place my Christian identity low down the list of allegiances I possess, coming a distant fourth to my football team, nationality and occupation, and make no attempt to let it be known that I am a Christian, or that I believe the gospel to be true. If I do, then it might reasonably be concluded that I don't really believe the gospel to be true for everyone – it is just true for me. So the question of whether Christians are prepared to be more public about their faith, to adopt a more conscious and open sense of Christian identity, is a crucial one for the survival of Christianity in the West, and for painting a new picture of Christian life as a serious lifestyle choice, not a casual brand allegiance.

Public Christianity

The interviewees reported in this book had a largely negative image of Christianity. However, when they did meet a real, live Christian, it was more often than not a positive experience. When they recalled actual Christians they had encountered, the image was much more positive than the general 'feel' conjured up by the idea of 'official Christianity'. Out of a greater sense of Christian identity needs to emerge a willingness to be less embarrassed about our Christianity, to ensure that such encounters with real Christians are frequent, positive and noticed.

Travelling on a train recently, surrounded by a large number of commuters heading out of London, I found myself thinking about how many of these people went anywhere near a church, or knew anything about Christ. They all seemed on the surface at least, ordinary, regular secular people going about their normal lives. As these thoughts were playing around my head, and thinking I was surely the only Christian on the train, I noticed that the person sitting opposite me – a man in his twenties, well turned out, apparently quite normal, healthy and not especially odd – took out a Bible and began to read it. Suddenly, the scene took on a new light. I began to wonder how many others of those in the carriage were also Christians. I began to feel ashamed of how I sometimes tend to keep the cover out of sight when reading a Christian book on a train. Here was an ordinary follower of Jesus, prepared in a very simple and unobtrusive way to be public about his Christianity.

One person interviewed for this book described how he had found being subjected to a long conversation about God while on a bus profoundly objectionable:

I had the misfortune to sit next to a guy on a bus, you know, and he just starts, just talking to me about Christ and all this stuff, and I'm thinking, 'Oh dear God, let there not be a traffic jam.'

Being buttonholed by some religious zealot and bombarded with questions when you can't escape is a pretty uncomfortable experience for most of us and we can perhaps sympathize. The observation was once made that 'People who want to share their religious views with you almost never want you to share yours with them.' Yet there is a great difference between pressing our views on others against their will, and simply being unashamedly public about our faith, in ways that don't force them on anyone. Wearing a cross on a lapel, saying that you went to church when asked what you did at the weekend, mentioning that prayer is one of the main ways you handle problems, dropping into a conversation the project you're working on with your local cell group to do gardening in elderly people's houses – these are all small things, and don't have to be followed by intensive interrogation of your interlocutor's religious beliefs, yet they make Christian faith visible.

Many Christians feel uncomfortable about explaining their faith, trying to steer conversations around to a discussion about the atonement. Even if they did want to, they are not quite sure how they would do it anyway. The fact is that if most of us were to live public Christian lives, making no apology for being a Christian, being willing to let it be known that we were followers of Christ and performing Christian discipleship in public, then we might be surprised at the reactions we receive. Sometimes it might bring ridicule or even persecution. When Daniel insisted on continuing to pray visibly at his window, even when such a public show of religion was banned under Nebuchadnezzar, such action was seen as subversive to the state and he soon found himself staring into the jaws of several hungry lions (Daniel 6:10–16). On other occasions such a public show of faith can lead to interesting conversations. The church at Philippi began when Paul and his friends simply went to the regular place of prayer on the Sabbath. In the course of the visit, a conversation started with a businesswoman named Lydia, which in turn led to her conversion and the planting of a new church.[7]

We are talking here about unashamed public acts of allegiance to Christ. This is not deliberate attention seeking, but simply refusing to live the Christian life in secret, and rejecting the secular insistence that Christian faith must be a private, not public, matter. An increasingly aggressive secularism may lead to any public show of allegiance to any religion being considered unlawful. So be it. Christianity has always claimed to be a public matter with social and political implications, not a private set of rituals performed behind closed doors. Public Christianity may lead to evangelism; it may lead to persecution. The task of Christians is not to be aggressive and obnoxious, but open and public about their faith, and leave the reactions of others in the hands of God.

Being prepared to be known as a Christian will lead to much more frequent encounters such as the ones outlined in the previous chapter – people actually recognizing real Christians in their midst who confound the stereotypes and drawing appropriate conclusions about them. If this principle were to be allied to the kind of pro-active Christian goodness outlined in the last section, its influence on public perceptions of Christianity could be huge.

Local action

However, all this will be fruitless if the common perception of Christians is that they talk a lot but don't make much difference. In recent years it is remarkable how enquiry courses like Alpha, Emmaus and Christianity Explored have sprung up in the churches of the UK and beyond. The biggest of these, the Alpha course, is now run in over 7,000 churches in the UK, in 155 countries world-wide, and 1.6 million British people are estimated to have taken part in an Alpha course. As a scheme for getting evangelism on to the agenda in the local church it has been an unparalleled success. A less well-known project coming from the same stable as Alpha is an organization called 'The Besom'. The idea behind it is to encourage Christians and churches to become involved in their local communities to do something to 'sweep away suffering'. Its simple self-description is, 'The Besom helps people make a difference. It provides a bridge between those who want to give time, money, things or skills and those who are in need. It ensures what is given is used effectively. The service it provides is free.'[8]

A Besom project might typically involve painting a flat for an elderly person, sorting clothing to be given to the homeless, getting involved in running a centre for victims of domestic violence, or helping resource a refugee family recently moved into the country. It simply provides the links to enable typical Christians who want to do something practical as an expression of their faith, to do so.

There are, of course, other agencies that do such work.[9] The point is this: imagine the difference it would make if as many churches as run Alpha courses also took on at least one ongoing project in their local community to offer down-to-earth practical help to the needy. This isn't, of course, to replace Alpha with such things, or to suggest that practical service is more important than evangelism. In fact, the two feed off each other and belong together. If Christian compassion is theologically more at home with missiology than soteriology, or, in other words, if we act with Christian goodness in the world so that others might 'see your good deeds and glorify our Father in heaven', then churches need to do both.

If churches began to be known as much for their practical action as for their evangelism, if church after church were recognized as being the best thing in their local communities because of the difference they make to life there, the image of Christianity in this country would slowly but surely change. A thought-provoking question to be asked of any local church is this: 'If your church vanished overnight, would anyone notice any difference?' This doesn't, of course, have anything to do with the question of whether anyone would notice if the building vanished – presumably the sudden disappearance of the Gothic pile at the end of the street might cause some consternation. The question refers to the Christian community. Would anyone's life suddenly lack something tangible or intangible? Would the local community notice the absence of support for the unemployed, comfort for the bereaved, healing for the broken or companionship for the elderly?

If churches took on this agenda with as much seriousness as they have begun to take on programmes like Alpha, their Alpha courses might themselves begin to be much fuller than they are at present. Allied to a greater sense of Christian identity, and a willingness to live public Christian lives, it could make all the difference for the public reputation of Christians in the UK. It could redefine and recapture the word 'Christian', and change its meaning.

Notes to Chapter 6

1. The full speech can be found at:
   http://www.bbc.co.uk/pressoffice/speeches/stories/thompson_livery.s
   html.

2. Of course, Jesus also says in the Sermon on the Mount, 'Do not do your
   acts of righteousness before men to be seen by them' (Matthew 6:1). The
   apparent contradiction between this and Mathew 5:16 can be resolved by
   considering the motivation for letting such behaviour become visible. In
   5:16, Jesus recommends that good deeds should be made visible so that
   they may 'praise your Father in heaven'. In 6:1 he counsels against such
   public action with the aim 'to be seen by men'. The question is, who is
   glorified by good deeds: God or me?

3. Adapted from J. Stevenson (ed.), *A New Eusebius: Documents Illustrative of
   the History of the Church to AD 337* (SPCK, 1957).

4. Galatians 2:11. Paul vehemently opposed Peter's practice in Antioch of
   refusing to eat with Gentile Christians, as a betrayal of this very principle.
   Peter's actions implied that being Jewish came before allegiance to Christ.

5. Lesslie Newbigin, *The Gospel in a Pluralist Society* (SPCK, 1989).

6. Ibid., p. 126.

7. Acts 16:13–15.

8. More information is on the Besom website: www.besom.com.

9. Faithworks is another organization dedicated to similar aims, 'working
   towards empowering and inspiring individual Christians and every local
   church to develop their role at the hub of their community'. See
   www.faithworks.info.

SECTION 4 | **CHURCH**

Of the many criticisms levelled at the institutional church, the most significant and damning is that it is self-referential and unnecessary. A faithful response to these criticisms would require the church to embrace a more incarnational idea of church issues. This would be responsive to people's questions, doubts and desires, connect with everyday life and provide the doctrinal, moral and spiritual resources to help people to live well.

7. UNNECESSARY CHURCH

Church attendance figures have become the accepted means of measuring Christianity's health in the UK. Every time the Church of England or Christian Research publish data that report a fall in weekly attendance, the familiar ecclesiastical death notices are published, and the familiar choruses of wailing or rejoicing grace newspaper editorials. As some of these editorials point out, it makes not a jot of difference that 40 million people call themselves Christian in national surveys if fewer than one in ten of them actually does anything about it.

Although it would be wrong to treat church-going as the *sole* measure of the Christian faith in the country, attendance figures are undeniably important. The claim that Christianity is about 'so much more than bums on seats' is a poor excuse. If people can't even be bothered to put their bums on the seats, they are unlikely to do 'so much more'. People may believe in God, like to appropriate the Christian label and even attend church for special occasions, but as an indication of the vitality of the gathered body of Christ, church attendance figures are hard to beat.

As everyone knows, levels of regular church attendance have been falling precipitously over recent years. Although difficult to measure with absolute precision, it seems that whereas around 11% of the population could be found in church on an average Sunday in 1980, that figure had dropped to 8% by 2000.[1] This decline is dramatic and sounds all the more so when you realize it is the equivalent of around 1,200 people leaving church every Sunday for two decades and not coming back.

It is worth noting, if only in passing, that this is not just a recent problem. In 1957, 14% of adults said they had been to church on the previous Sunday.[2] Ten years before that, a Mass Observation report recorded that

> Both in regard to formal observances and general attitude, the younger generation show a much more critical outlook, and much less interest [in religion]. Two young people (under forty) express doubt about the existence of God for every older person who does so. It is mostly the younger generation who dismiss religion with apparent disinterest.[3]

Thirty years before that, a survey of the religious attitudes of trench soldiers in the First World War revealed a disturbingly familiar picture:

> [The soldiers had the impression] that there is little or no life in the Church at all, that it is an antiquated and decaying institution, standing by dogmas expressed in archaic language, and utterly out of touch with modern thought and living experience . . . they believe that the Churches are more and more governed by the middle-aged and the elderly; they think ministry professionalised and out of touch with the life of men, deferring unduly to wealth . . . They say they do not see any real differences in the strength and purity of life between the people who go to church and the people who do not.[4]

It is also worth noting, by means of mitigation, that the church, and in particular the Church of England, has a vast fringe constituency. It baptizes around a fifth of all newborn babies, marries around a third of all wedding couples and officiates at nearly all funerals. The church sees an estimated third of the population attending at least one service at some point in the average year. The number of non-infant baptisms actually increased in the 1990s and some process

evangelism courses, most notably Alpha, have achieved both prom-
inence and a measure of success.

Having said all that, the obituary notices seem to have got it about
right and Cardinal Cormac Murphy O'Connor's unfortunate remark
that Christianity was 'almost vanquished' in Britain has almost become
the leitmotiv of the new century. Some of the reasons have been
explored in other chapters of this book – people's privatized attitude
to God and spirituality, their culturally shaped intellectual difficulties
with Christian claims, their misunderstanding and/or misuse of the
label 'Christian' – but perhaps the most important one is the same one
that was articulated by British soldiers in the trenches eighty years ago:
attending church has little discernible impact on people's lives.

Being an institution

The most important social fact about the church is that it is an institution, and institutions are deeply unpopular in modern Britain. Much
in the same way, as we saw in Chapter 5, that the word 'religious' has
become almost redundant as an adjective, 'institutional' is now almost
a term of abuse, encapsulating the very opposite of the individualized,
autonomous freedom we so cherish.

Social surveys show that we (claim to) trust and respect the monar-
chy, Parliament, the judiciary, the police and even the army far less
today than we did twenty years ago. In as far as the church is an institution – and it is certainly perceived to be one – it has suffered in a
similar manner.

Institutions constrict, limiting personal freedom and placing
demands on individual lifestyles, prioritizing the whole over its parts,
and insisting on the loyalty that is the prerequisite of serious belonging. Over the last forty years, the British attitude and response to this
exacting and rather arduous form of belonging has changed
significantly. We marry less, and cohabit and divorce more. We are
less inclined to join political organizations, trade unions and local
community groups. We have shallower community roots, travelling
further to work, shop, school and relax, and moving house more frequently. We spend more time in our cars than we do on foot, and
know our neighbours and neighbourhood rather less well than previous generations did. The lifelong employer and career are, for most
people, a thing of the past. In as far as the church is a locally rooted

organization to which individuals are expected to attend and belong, it suffers.

These contextual, cultural trends have combined to impact our church-going habits. Whereas once respectability, social standing and even personal advancement required regular church attendance, today individualism, consumerism, anti-institutionalism and rootlessness all discourage it. None of this should, however, be used to excuse the church for falling attendance figures. The 'institution' may have suffered for cultural reasons outside its control, but it has also suffered for not having listened to what people are saying about it.

As mentioned in the Introduction, listening to people does not necessarily entail obeying them. Twenty-first-century, postmodern, culturally sensitive Britons may dislike the idea of the uniqueness of Christ, but jettisoning that teaching to please them is not an option for the church. Similarly, when interviewees explain that, to appeal to them, the church should be '[full] of people, despite what their beliefs [are]' or that '[they should] knock the cross down [and] make it more modern [and] user-friendly', the right to ignore advice becomes a positive necessity.

Much of what people had to say about the church was factually dubious, based less on personal experience than on reputation, report and rumour. Some of it was spiced with real venom. Such opinions may invalidate themselves as serious advice, but that does not make them irrelevant. True or not, biased or not, the fact that church and church-going were perceived negatively is both significant and damaging.

Predictable . . . and boring

Many of the criticisms levelled at the church will not surprise the reader. It was considered oppressively didactic, a relic of a more deferential society in which people were told how they should think and behave. 'I personally don't like being told what to think or what I should think,' one female student said. Rather than offering a forum for discussion, 'It tells you and you listen and [then] go home.' It is 'dogmatic' and 'patriarchal', built around antiquated 'rites and rituals'. 'It pays lip service to creative thinking.'

Church services are dull and anodyne, 'predictable . . . [and] boring', events to which you 'just pay lip service, standing up and sitting down at the right time, [while everything] is just happening around you.' They are uncomfortable, 'cold [and] long' events during which 'you sit on hard benches'. They could be unfriendly and intimidating, especially to newcomers.

As an institution, church was inflexible and absolutist. 'They want you to have the whole package . . . and even if you only want a part of their lifestyle or a part of their beliefs, they are not willing.' It is unwilling or unable to handle 'doubt and uncertainty', and masquerades its questionable beliefs as facts.

'Within the church there is a constant scratching around or looking for some definite answers,' one middle-aged woman said. 'I think it is very unrealistic,' she continued. 'It is the sort of thinking that comes out of children and in a way it appeals to people out there who are finding life difficult. It is rubbish because at the end of the day it is still a matter of faith. What the church has done is say, "We know this to be true" [whereas] we can only say that we think we know it is true.'

There were opinions of the church that disagreed with some of these sentiments and by no means all interviewees were hostile either to the church or to the experience of church-going. However, many of these examples often simply underlined how deficient the 'usual' experience is.

'If it is somewhere like St John's,' one young woman said of her local church, 'with banners up and is quite modern, [it] has a real vibe about it and has people my own age, then it is connected with normal society. [That's] great, it makes me feel elated, alive and there's a real energy and a loving atmosphere. But often you go into places, orthodox churches or whatever, and they are beautiful buildings, but boring.'

Unnecessary and self-referential
As observed, many of these criticisms will be familiar to readers. Some appear to be justifiable; others, based on prejudice or simply personal taste. Underlying many of them, however, and at the heart of the problem that people had with church was that it was simply unnecessary. This was for two reasons.

The first one relates to an area that we touched upon in Chapter 1, the privatization of God. This went hand in hand with his democratization. Whereas once upon a time (and rather more recently than at the Reformation, in the eyes of interviewees), the church was the mediator between God and the people, it no longer had that role. Time and time again, respondents declared, often in wholly sincere ways, that they did not go to church 'because I have got God anyway'.

'Not going to church . . . does not mean you're not a Christian. It's what you do in life that matters,' explained one interviewee, touching on the divided definitions of 'Christian' that were noted in Chapter 5. 'Standing in a garage makes you no more a car than going to church makes you a Christian,' reasoned another. 'If you believe in God you must believe that he is everywhere and can hear you, so you don't need to go to a church,' said a third. 'You don't have to be there if he is everywhere,' echoed a fourth.

This attitude to church – that it was unnecessary because God was available to everyone directly, without the need of any mediation – was perhaps most evident in people's attitudes to prayer. As noted in Chapter 1, there was a somewhat surprising amount of communicating with God going on among the hesitant theists, self-confessed agnostics, and hardened atheists who were interviewed. Crucially important for these relationships, however, was the fact that conversations had to be *on people's own terms* and *according to their own needs*. Prayer was not made prayer by being uttered in a certain place, among certain people or according to a certain pattern. A small handful of elderly interviewees expressed the sense that prayer was aided by being in locations 'where prayer has been valid', but for the vast majority, church was simply not necessary for prayer.

Interviewees said things like, 'You *can* go to church and worship but I believe anybody can pray to God and that is why I don't necessarily go to church every week', or 'I don't think there is any specific place where you are meant to communicate with him.' Indeed, in a faint, if unconscious, echo of Matthew 6:6, one young woman said that prayer could quite easily be in your bedroom, unseen, with the door closed:

> I used to go [to church] quite often but quite often if I really feel that I need guidance or want to say a prayer I will quite often do it upstairs in my bedroom.

Such prayer had the advantage of efficiency. 'You can pray in the garden but you can't do the gardening in a church,' as one interviewee pithily expressed it. It also ran close to the gentle, non-committal contemplative life that interviewees tended to favour.

'I choose a place outside alone just to sit and think,' one young man recounted in an interesting and candid moment that underlined the point that genuinely spiritual moments need not take place within church walls:

> I can say there have been a few times when I have felt that I have been connected to something bigger than myself. It did happen just for a split second . . . and I just felt as if I had jumped up higher and could see everything for a split second and then come straight back down and then it is forgotten. I can't explain it at all. Whether that was the touch of God in some form I don't know.

The result of this democratization of God, prayer and spiritual experiences was that church was simply rendered unnecessary.

The second reason for church's redundancy was that, as far as most interviewees were concerned, church and church-going was effectively *about itself.* Many of the criticisms levelled at the church (didactic, patriarchal, boring etc.) also constituted a subtle critique of the content and language of church-going, meaning its form and rituals as well as it vocabulary. As noted in Chapter 1, people did have real and sometimes pressing questions about purpose, destiny, morality, God and other spiritual matters. In as far as the interviewees understood some of the traditional Christian responses to these, they had some problems with them, but those problems were exacerbated by the ways in which the responses to these questions were (perceived to be) articulated in church.

Sometimes the criticisms were direct. 'The other thing is "he cometh unto me . . ." Oh, the language!' one middle-aged woman exclaimed. More commonly, there was simply general incomprehension of how 'the classic service of hymns, sermons and readings' was supposed to encourage me in my spiritual quest or help me live my life. The whole experience seemed to be predominantly self-referential rather than about the big metaphysical issues that, in fact, underpinned it.

The same criticism could be applied to the Christians who attended church, a point that does not surprise after the comments in Chapter 5. 'I just feel that people that are religious . . . they are very self-centred and they just want to talk about themselves and they are on about religion all the time and they are rarely interested in other people,' one young woman complained.

Either way, the underlying accusation was that the experience failed to connect with the 'here and now' or 'the bigger picture'. 'The story behind it all just doesn't interest me at all . . . [I'm interested in] what I believe about here and now . . .' one interviewee said. 'I don't think that in this day and age people want religion rammed down their throats. They want it as part of a bigger picture,' said another.

Listening to the world

It is important to emphasize that none of these criticisms in itself necessitates that the church must change. Many criticisms were made from a standpoint of ignorance and some from one of malice. Most were profoundly if unconsciously shaped by the cultural and intellectual air that interviewees breathed, in much the same way as were the intellectual criticisms explored in Chapter 3.

Hence, an unconsciously consumerist perspective resulted in the church being evaluated as just another consumer service provider. 'The church should reflect what we want,' one middle-aged woman said. 'The church should not dictate to us that you can get married, you can't get married. We want to get married. We are consumers of the church.' An aggressively postmodern, egalitarian and anti-elitist perspective condemned the preacher for no reason other than disliking the fact that he engaged in the act of teaching. 'I don't like this sermon thing,' one interviewee said, 'because it's that one person's way of interpreting whatever he read. It's not a group discussion . . . it's just him telling you.'

When faced with this kind of 'advice', the judicious response is, of course, to treat it with extreme caution or to ignore it altogether. Yet, to reiterate the premise of this book, this should not become an excuse to disregard all uncomfortable criticisms of church and church-going, nor to reject all awkward advice. Crass as some advice may have been, much of what people said about the church is genuinely valuable, if not always easy to hear.

An example of this can be seen in the number of interviewees who made the point, albeit obliquely, that the physical environment of the church and its services should reflect the basic tenets of Christianity or else risk confusing and alienating visitors. Strangers to a church see the message long before they hear the message. A story of love, joy, hope, reconciliation and life sounds somewhat unconvincing if the appearance, welcome, temperature, atmosphere, format and nature of the service is unkempt, cold, unfriendly, tired, rigid, incomprehensible and joyless. Running such a painful gauntlet before hearing a sermon inevitably frames and determines the message of that sermon, irrespective of what is actually said in it. No amount of pulpit pyrotechnics will hide the fact that the good news has not been *embodied* in the church experience. Accordingly, interviewees said that church needed 'to be comfortable and not cold . . . a bit more social'. 'There should be large sitting-rooms . . . and coffee . . . it's got to be a sanctuary . . . forgiving . . . peaceful . . . equal.'

On one level, these were simply consumerist comments, driven by people's experience of rebranding campaigns and high street store makeovers. Yet, they are no less acute for having their origins in the commercial world, implying, as the following quotation does, that a more 'worshipper-friendly' physical atmosphere can actually embody the spiritual truths that are supposed to be communicated in the service and help people in their everyday lives. In spite of the determined egalitarianism in what this student had to say – an egalitarianism that saw church as essentially a mutual therapy session – his final comment is particularly alert and poignant:

> A church service automatically brings in the thought of, that you have got to go in, sit down, all go to such and such a hymn, then you will do this, do that and then it is half past eleven and almost finishing. It is all very formal. It would be nice to see it as an open microphone session, people using everyone else in the church as their counselling medium, asking questions, and very much on a less formal basis . . . a place to heal what the working week has taken out of you.

As several other interviewees said more directly, church services should not demand that people fit into a predetermined programme but should rather develop their innate spirituality. They should 'help people connect with their spiritual self . . . drawing their own inner wisdom out'. Even more pointedly, they 'should be much more about meeting and discussing and trying to learn and find enjoyment and pleasure in trying to develop one's spirituality . . . [an opportunity] to develop yourself into the person, if there is a God, that he wants you to be'.

As ever, such advice needs to be handled with care, and it is interesting that even some of the interviewees recognized this. 'It can't be all things to all people,' one young woman said. 'Whilst you have to be tolerant of people, you just can't make it into something like a night out,' said another.

Such caution noted, however, it is worth concluding with the frequency of calls for the church to adapt and play a vital role in community and society – many of which were clearly underpinned by a good will that was deep-rooted, in spite of the widespread and sometimes aggressive criticism. In their own way, they echoed the words quoted in the Introduction that 'given the orthodoxy of the grow-earn-spend philosophy, the case for the church . . . to act as counter-culture has never been stronger'.

Church, interviewees said, needs to be a 'place where you can [find] comfort and help people and guide them in the right direction', a place 'to build a community, warmth, belonging, hope'. It needs 'to adapt in terms of . . . how people celebrate God and worship', with one interviewee commenting positively, 'I think it is lovely that they now have places for children because at one time if you were little in church it was awful.'

It needs to be 'always open and welcoming, [no] matter who you are', a place that 'lets people know that there is always something there for you to come [to] and to express how you feel and tell people about your problems and not be judged in any way, shape or form, no matter what you have done'.

It should be 'a centre that is meeting the needs of the community but also offering sanctuary for those who want it', a place that 'tries [to] bring the community together with different activities', a 'place of comfort, solace, fun, a place to be respected, a place that reaches out, [that] goes to the people'.

It should be an organization that will 'nurture the young [and] give them a sense of respect and love for others without forcing it down their throats'. 'Its role should be to bring spiritual knowledge and sustenance and a strong sense of morality to public affairs.'

'It should be happy and informative,' one young man said, recalling that 'I have seen things that have inspired me, like these churches where you see people dancing around in the aisles and singing from the soul.' 'What [after all] is worshipping God?' he continued perceptively. 'Is it not a celebration of what is good, [of] all positive things, singing from the heart and singing together?'

Notes to Chapter 7

1. See Christian Research, *Religious Trends*.
2. MORI, *British Public Opinion Newsletter*, summer 2003.
3. *Puzzled People: A Study in Popular Attitudes to Religion, Ethics, Progress and Politics in a London Borough. Prepared for the Ethical Union by Mass Observation* (Victor Gollancz, 1947).
4. D. S. Cairns (ed.), *The Army and Religion* (Macmillan, 1919), quoted in Robin Gill, *The Myth of the Empty Church* (SPCK, 1993).

8. FRUITFUL THEOLOGY

Of all the critiques listed in the last chapter, one stands out as the most telling. It is the charge that the church is wrapped up in itself. To many on the outside, it seems that it is an institution fascinated and consumed by its own life and activities, walled-up and enclosed. The language, ritual and practice all make sense (supposedly) within the church, but don't mean much to the casual outsider. The result of this is a double impenetrability. Such an institution becomes difficult to penetrate from the outside – hence the bemusement of some observers trying to make sense of what might or might not be happening in church. At the same time, though, it becomes difficult for people within the church to break out. In other words, those involved in church life and activity often find themselves in a whirl of meetings, services and sermons, which have very little to do with anything they do outside church. Hence, their life and practice outside church are rarely affected by anything they do inside church. Marriages move on, money is spent, mortgages are paid, children are raised, with little, if any, noticeable difference from those who do not go to church at all.

Many of the other critiques of church mentioned in the previous chapter flow from this same sense of self-referentiality. The idea that it is overly *dogmatic* reflects a sense that it simply states its own opinions without any intention of discussion, dialogue, interaction or questioning (this may or may not be true of church these days, but the fact that this is how it is perceived remains significant).

The criticism that the church is *unnecessary* is a two-edged sword. On the one hand, it reflects the individualism of an atomized culture that was mentioned in Chapter 2. Of course church will seem unnecessary if we believe that basically we do not need each other, or at least we do not need those who are different from us. However, there is still a nagging truth in this criticism that needs hearing. This notion, closely tied to the belief that it is perfectly possible to be a good person, believe in God and have a spiritual life without darkening the doors of a church, reflects the thought that what goes on in church will most likely be completely useless for the actual task of living life.

The issue is not so much whether church connects with issues that non-Christians face, as whether it connects with issues that its own members face. It doesn't matter whether you are a Christian or not, you still have to run relationships, live in families, face disappointment, manage finances, go to work, vote and the like. The question is whether anything in church might affect the way you went about those tasks and roles. And the common perception is that it doesn't.

Now of course, how true this is will vary from church to church. It will be more true of some than others. Some churches will have quite a strong sense of relevance and frequently address issues that people face all the time. Others will feel entirely disconnected from anything in the world outside, and may well be among those accelerating the figures of decline in church attendance. If this is the case, there is a key theological problem at the root of the issue – a failure to grasp the incarnational nature of Christian communication.

Incarnation, the church and the world

Few churches explicitly deny the incarnation. There are a few on the liberal fringe of the church who think Jesus was after all just a prophet, but by and large, it is taken as a given of historic Christian faith that Jesus of Nazareth is the divine Son of God, the Word Incarnate, the second person of the Trinity. However, it is one thing to acknowledge the truth of this article of Christian doctrine. It is another to live it. It is one thing to recite it in creeds, Sunday after Sunday. It is another to express it in the very fabric of a local church, to have incarnation breathe through its rhythms of daily life and relationship.

The incarnation – the Word become flesh – is the point at which God and the world he has created meet. It is the place where God's very being intersects with the physical world we live in, and the place where we get to see what God looks like in human form. It is where God cooks food, has conversations, drinks wine, talks about work, politics and sex, and dies on a Roman cross.

It is also where the physical world is taken up into God. Here, human life is given a dignity and worth it didn't quite have before, because God has shared it. When you visit older English towns, you often come across ancient pubs that display a sign outside, mentioning the fact that some king or famous personage once stayed in this inn for a night. That is its claim to fame, its proud boast. This physical world we live in, and in particular humanity within it, bears a similar sign, makes a similar boast that God once stayed here. The fact that God became human, that he lived an ordinary (although also extraordinary) human life, means that human life now has a significance that it did not have before. It is dignified, honoured – if you belong to the human race, then you are privileged to be part of a species in which God chose to make his home.[1] More than that, though – lest we feel this privileges us over other parts of creation – it is important to remember that although it is true in a special way of humanity, it is also true for the rest of the creation, which humanity is called to look after and care for in God's name.

Sometimes Christianity is seen as 'other-worldly', and church as a welcome respite from ordinary life, a means of escape from the harsh world outside. The problem is that the incarnation won't let you do that. It won't allow you to wrap up God far away from the real world, too pure to be touched by it. Without the incarnation, it would be fair to encourage an idea of church as a kind of spiritual escape, a place for all things heavenly, pure and immaterial, far away from the realities of trying to live life. Yet the Word became *flesh* – real, normal, human flesh – and hence God is connected into and committed to his world irrevocably.

In Jesus, God lived a real human life with all its frustrations and limitations. God connected with the world in real and not imaginary ways. In the same way, a fully incarnational church will have all kinds of connections with 'real life'. It will be the kind of community in which you constantly see a new way of looking at things and a new way of doing things – it will be a place where you are not encouraged to escape life, but where you can learn a new way of living it. It will not lead you out of the real world and into a different, 'spiritual' one – it will take you back into the real world with new eyes and ears and a new heart.

This has a number of implications for the church today as it tries to listen hard to what outsiders are saying and to God as he speaks to us.

Christian communication: the content

Many of the interviewees whose opinions are recorded in these pages thought the church too dogmatic. In one sense, we shouldn't be too worried by such a criticism. Whether we like the word or not,[2] Christian faith does have certain dogmas, doctrines or core beliefs, as does any other religion, political position or philosophy. Yet the substance of the criticism is about the way in which those dogmas are held. It refers to the sense that doctrine or theology is basically about abstract statements that are required to be believed without question or argument, and that, bearing in mind what we have just been discussing, are essentially unconnected with 'life'.

The issue here is the role of theology. Sometimes (and it is not at all clear whether this view is held more widely inside or outside the church) theology is thought to be about a set of ideas which are there to help you get your ideas right. This is 'Truth' with a capital T, and you had better believe it. Now this is certainly not to claim that theology does not concern Truth. Christian theology is itself a response to God's revelation of himself in Christ as the Way, the Truth and the Life. However, it is an inadequate and unchristian view of theology to understand it merely as abstract, impartial, disembodied truth. The purpose of Christian theology is not simply to help us think right; it is there to help us live right. It is meant to be fruitful, not barren. This is the central point of Ellen Charry's excellent book *By the Renewing of Your Minds*.[3] Her argument goes that the theologians of the classic Christian tradition would have been horrified by the idea that Christian doctrine was some abstract philosophical game, played by Christian intellectuals to pass the time, or even to solve some tricky metaphysical problems. Instead, the whole point of Christian theology is to help us live excellent human lives. As she puts it while discussing Basil of Caesarea:

> Liturgical language teaches correct knowledge of God, and knowing God is the only way to reach the goal of human life: to become as God-like as possible . . . The Christian life is a tutorial in holiness.[4]

True human happiness comes from knowing God. And to know God, we need Christian doctrine. The function of Christian doctrine is to enable us to know who God is, who we are, to find our true place in the universe and thus to find true happiness and to live well. If we know who we are and what kind of place this world is, it will also begin to show us how we are to live in the world. It will show us what is of true value and what is of little worth. It will help us make wise choices in how we spend our money, give guidance to our children, and treat each other.

When one interviewee said that 'It's what you *do* that matters', they were half right. Yes, living right is vital. The purpose of the gospel is to conform us to God – forgiven, reconciled, restored, becoming like him (Ephesians 4:24) and doing what he would do. Its purpose is in one sense to make us live well in this world as an anticipation of the new heavens and the new earth, which will one day come about. Yet we can learn how to live rightly only if we know the purpose for which we are made. You might take a violin and use it to play tennis or to scratch that annoying itch halfway down your back. However, only when it is in the hands of a master, being used for the purpose for which it was created – making beautiful music – does it come into its own. Only when we know who and what we are, and the purpose for which we were made, can we really begin to learn how to live rightly and how to treat each other. This is what Christian doctrine and dogma are: an account of who God is, who we are, and of the purpose of human life, given to enable us to live rightly in God's world.

Learning from the early Christians

In the first few centuries of the Christian church, to become a Christian was not something you just chose to do one Sunday morning

by turning up at church. The usual practice was to join the catechumenate, a long-term commitment to undergo Christian instruction.
This could last several years, and the teaching consisted of several
aspects. The catechumen would be expected to attend church, at least
up to the point when the eucharistic liturgy began, when, after a bless-
ing, they would be politely shown the door – that part was only for the
fully baptized. During the section of the service at which they were
present, catechumens would listen to the reading of the Bible and to
its steady exposition. In addition, catechumens would sometimes
listen to a series of lectures explaining basic Christian doctrine.[5] In this
way, doctrinal knowledge was built up in the new believers, to provide
a foundation for their new life and practice.

Another key part of their instruction was some detailed moral
teaching about appropriate Christian behaviour. The *Didache* (literally
'The Teaching', an early Christian writing, probably from the first
century, and the kind of literature that comes out of this stable)
begins with the bold statement 'There are two Ways: a Way of Life
and a Way of Death, and the difference between these two Ways is
great.'[6] The work then proceeds to spell out in pretty bold detail what
Christians do and don't do and why. Christians will give generously
when asked. They will avoid magic, astrology, abortion and sexual
promiscuity. Christian masters will speak gently to slaves, slaves will
respect and obey masters as representatives of God. They will be
cautious about entertaining lust, wanting to be rich or feelings of
hatred for people, however bad. We wouldn't always agree with all the
detail, as culturally it is a very different setting to ours, yet it is strik-
ing how 'applied' this teaching is. It leaves the enquirer in no doubt
as to the new way of life they are being invited to enter.[7]

In addition to all this, the catechumen was to be given specific
instruction on the kinds of spiritual practices that were intended to
root these patterns of behaviour deep into the fabric of these new
believers' lives. They were taught about prayer, attendance at
worship, coming under the teaching of the Scriptures, and regular
participation in the Eucharist, when the time came. The second part
of the *Didache*, after the focused instruction on Christian behaviour,
is precisely this – a manual for spiritual formation. It tells you when
to fast, how to pray, how to listen to Christian teaching, how to
respond to prophecy and so on.

The early church understood the way Christian teaching works. They understood that these three kinds of teaching – doctrinal, moral and spiritual – are needed to both ground Christians in their faith, and prevent it from becoming abstract, irrelevant and over-dogmatic. Churches today could do a lot worse than follow this threefold pattern as they think about and plan the process of Christian education.

Doctrinal teaching
There is no substitute for basic catechetical teaching. Perhaps one of the significant things that the Alpha course has brought to the church worldwide is not just the evangelistic edge it adds for the conversion of those outside the church, but also the way it has provided a catechetical tool for teaching the basics of the faith – after all, most churches running Alpha for the first time find the course is largely filled with existing church-people, who may never have gone through a course of teaching in basic Christianity before. However it is done, whether through Alpha or another means, the purpose of this kind of teaching is to help Christians understand the story of the Bible and the basic meaning of such doctrines as Trinity, creation, fall, redemption, incarnation, atonement and eschatology – the doctrines that the classic creeds recount.

In connection with this, churches often make two mistakes. One is to think that lay people are incapable of understanding such theology and so they need simple anecdotes, inspirational stories or moral instruction. That, however, is to take a disastrous short cut. There is little point in inspirational stories before we have understood what inspired them in the first place. Moral instruction becomes mere legalism if it does not flow directly out of a theology of grace. It is also patronizing to lay Christians, who are often very capable of making good sense of such things if they are communicated well.

The other mistake is to think that this is all that Christians need. In this scenario, every sermon takes its subject matter as a particular Christian doctrine, or a specific passage of Scripture. The difficulty with this approach is that unless the expositor is particularly skilled, many of the issues that ordinary people have to grapple with daily – dealing with competition at work, ambition, making ends meet, buying a house and suchlike – may never get addressed at all. Instead, topics like church unity, prayer and the doctrine of sin will come up again and again – all very useful and important, but unless taken further, they will often fall short of helping Christians live Christian lives. To meet this need, there is another kind of teaching that needs to follow from basic catechesis.

Moral teaching

Christian education, through teaching and preaching, will also need to be much more intentional about helping Christian people to see how this set of beliefs works out in the daily practice of contemporary life, and the kinds of patterns of behaviour that flow from these beliefs. This kind of teaching will take topics like parenting, debt, busyness, poverty and sex (the equivalent of astrology, pagan worship and slave–master relationships in the early church) and explore how Christians might act in the daily encounter with these issues. This might be in a series of sermons or seminars, or Lent groups – the setting is less important than the need.

Without this kind of theological reflection on the practice of living contemporary life, Christian doctrine remains abstract, unconnected, remote – just like many of the people interviewed in this book felt church to be. If this is the *only* kind of Christian teaching on offer, then it will become prey to one of the other frequent critiques of church – that it is just a set of moralistic, dogmatic rules to be followed, with no reason or rationale given for why they matter. If we are to help our churches to become more incarnational, more able to embody the teachings of the faith in the actual practice of life, then Christian teachers will need to become more adept at this practice of theological reflection. It will mean developing and practising the ability to look at contemporary life in the light of God's revelation in Christ and the Scriptures, so that sermons are not always about specifically 'theological' subjects or an exposition of a particular text, but instead seek to apply a holistic biblical theology to concerns that ordinary people (not just Christians) face day after day.

Spiritual teaching

The process of induction of new Christians in the early church shows us yet another form of Christian instruction, which goes beyond basic teaching and applied reflection, to include spiritual formation. Very often maturity in Christian faith is measured by how well you can quote the Bible, or by how many church committees you sit on. In the New Testament churches, maturity would be more likely to be measured by the visibility of such qualities as goodness, kindness, generosity, humility and self-control. Again, this gives us a clue as to why church can often feel so self-absorbed from the outside, and so *unnecessary*. If the direction church points you in is purely a knowledge of its own internal belief system, or involvement in its own structures, it is not surprising if people both inside and outside the church feel that church doesn't contribute much of any great worth to the actual task of living.

Imagine, however, a church that was able to say to its local community, 'We can enable you to do the very things you need to do to survive life, build good relationships, and become a more fully human person. We can teach you forgiveness, love, trust, hope, generosity, hospitality, self-control. And the reason we can do this is because these describe the very character of the God we believe in.' Such a church might suddenly begin to find people in their locality beginning to pay attention – where else can you learn these vital life skills, which all people know they need if they are to be able to 'do life' successfully?

Increasing numbers of people spend their Sunday mornings not in church but in the gym. The reason they do this is simple. Gyms are local communities organized around and committed to the task of enabling people to acquire physical health and fitness. People join either because they feel unfit and sense that they need to become more healthy, or because they have seen a picture of a model with rippling muscles and a firm-toned body, and want their own to look exactly like that.

When you join, you are given a specific set of exercises that will slowly but surely help you to acquire physical health and fitness. You will be given specific programmes to work on your thighs, back, neck, biceps, stomach and so on. If you do the exercises stipulated, you will be able to do things you could not have done otherwise, like run up stairs without getting breathless, bend over without breaking your spine, or play tennis. You will feel better, live longer and become more physically attractive to others. The benefits are obvious, and the means are provided to achieve those benefits, and the result is that people join in their droves, paying increasing sums in subscriptions and much time and pain and effort to get what they know they need if they are to live well.

The comparison with church is instructive. Imagine church as a local community dedicated to cultivating the spiritual health and fitness of its members. Imagine a church that was dedicated to fostering such habits of life as generosity, forgiveness, patience or kindness. Imagine a church that worked towards developing not so much physical health, depicted in the firm muscles and taut skin of a model, but spiritual fitness, depicted in the beauty and character of Christ. It is instructive how often New Testament writers use physical exercise as a metaphor for spiritual growth: 'Train yourself to be godly. For physical training is of some value, but godliness has value for all things, holding promise for both the present life and the life to come' (1 Timothy 4:7–8).[8]

The point of all this is that if churches were able to focus their resources more directly, and gain a reputation for being able to teach people to acquire virtue – to become like Christ in developing the Christlike qualities of joy, peace, patience, kindness, goodness, faithfulness, gentleness and self-control (Galatians 5:22) – then they would go a long way towards reversing the reputation they have for being irrelevant, unnecessary and self-absorbed. They would be offering something that lies right at the theological heart of their mission – to enable people to become like Christ – and that at the same time chimes in with many people's yearnings to learn these crucial skills or arts of living that are so absent in our societies.

Now this spiritual formation is based in and arises out of the two other kinds of teaching mentioned above. The ability to forgive emerges out of a sense that you have been forgiven. The ability to be patient grows from a profound sense that God is the true judge who will bring things to a proper conclusion in his time, not mine.

Stanley Hauerwas argues that 'we have underwritten a voluntaristic conception of the Christian faith, which presupposed that one can become a Christian without training'.[9] Churches wanting to engage with this agenda will develop resources and practices designed to provide the kind of training that builds these very things as habits of life. This will involve teaching Christian doctrine so as to show the connections and roots of such patterns of life within the Christian faith. It will involve spiritual disciplines of prayer, fasting, meditation and study to dig deep roots of Christian character in the soul.

To sum up, churches will need to give greater attention to the whole programme of Christian education and communication than they have been accustomed to doing in the past. Gone are the days when people could be assumed to have picked up Christian faith and teaching with their mother's milk and from the general surrounding culture. Becoming a Christian means the renewing of mind, heart and outlook. It means gaining a new set of eyes to view the world, a new range of habits to acquire, a new way of life to live. Churches will need in particular to ensure that teaching and instruction covers these three vital areas of *doctrinal*, *moral* and *spiritual* formation if they are to offer something truly transforming and connected into the task of living – something truly incarnational.

Christian communication: the style

Another of the critiques that needs to be heard and weighed carefully is the idea that church demands 'all or nothing': 'They want you to have the whole package. And not all of us need that in our lives . . . So instead of you being able to dip in/dip out, they are not that flexible, I feel.' This is, of course, also connected to the belief that church just preaches at people and doesn't provide a more democratic forum where ideas or experiences can be shared and explored. In one sense, of course, these criticisms are shallow and pointless. To reduce church to a forum where people can just talk about their own thoughts and prejudices would make it just another social club and, frankly, quite boring, attractive only to those who have little better to do, and enjoy listening to their own voices. Without any clear set of ideas, beliefs and practices to engage with, such an enterprise would be no more than a talking shop. However, there is, as usual, a point behind these anxieties. They reflect a deep human desire to explore, to find oneself taken seriously, to learn by discovery rather than dictation.

The doctrine of the incarnation, as it was developed in the early church, tells us that when we think of God, we are to begin with Jesus. This means not starting with our own ideas and trying to fit Jesus in somewhere. Instead, it means allowing our understanding of God to be conformed to Christ. One of the very significant things about the incarnation is that in becoming flesh God makes himself available. We can interact with him, ask him questions, and find him asking questions back again. Coming through many of the interviews represented in this research is the image of God as the white-robed, bearded divine law-giver delivering the Ten Commandments to Moses on the mountain as a fait accompli. Moses is hardly likely to ask for time to discuss these with his colleagues, or the right to propose his own list.

Far less often do we think of God as he is in Christ, teaching by conversation, drawing things out of people by searching questions or stories, entering into debate and dialogue. It is not, of course, that Jesus has nothing to say, and no convictions to argue. He is not simply 'providing a space where people can discuss their ideas'. But neither does he pronounce dogmatically from a distance, allowing no interaction or counter-questioning. Instead, he takes the questions, desires and aspirations of the people he encounters with the utmost seriousness, however wrong-headed they may be. The woman who is fed up with doctors and comes to touch his cloak, hoping for healing by physical contact with this miracle man (Mark 5:25–34), is displaying little more than a superstitious desperation. Yet Jesus takes her seriously, accepts her credulity as faith and gives her the healing she longs for. Jesus' sermons are always interactive affairs. He will often tell a parable which draws out discussion and questions from his listeners. This process of interaction will then divide those who are genuinely interested and eager for God's truth from those who are casually amused by his presence, and just want to see a few miracles or spiritual pyrotechnics.[10]

The manner in which teaching is offered is to be determined by the incarnational nature of the faith as much as the content. Churches that echo the incarnational nature of the God they worship will address not just the content of teaching – its doctrinal, moral and spiritual core – but also the style in which it is done.

Several years ago, I spoke in a large Anglican church in Malaysia, where I was told I needed to prepare not just a sermon, but also a series of questions arising out of the sermon in time to go in the Sunday news-sheet, and which would then be discussed at the large number of midweek cell groups that constituted the core of the church. Group leaders then took copious notes of my sermon, so they could deliver the gist of it a few days later as they led their cell groups. The groups were then able to talk over the sermon and its ideas, and begin to ask how they might apply it in their own individual lives (it's easier to do that in small settings than for one preacher to try to provide detailed application for a wide range of people). It also sharpened this preacher's preparation, knowing that his sermon was to be dissected and discussed widely just a few days later!

One of the attractive and effective points of Alpha, and other enquiry courses that have followed its lead, is the embrace of group sessions where any question can be asked and is encouraged. Alpha, for example, aims to be a place where 'no question is too simple and no question too hostile'. Such an approach models precisely a combination of the core convictions that lie at the heart of Christian faith, with the openness to question, explore, discuss and interact that is at the heart of incarnational evangelism and that many people seem to want to find in church. It is not only pragmatically effective, it is also theologically appropriate: accepting and welcoming questions (and not just preaching at people) is exactly what God does in the Incarnation – he invites us to interact with him and question him. Jesus does not just preach at people from a safe distance, but he invited people to ask him questions, have conversations with him, even to dispute what he says, and thus come to discover the truth through the process.

However this might be modelled, it is vital that this kind of approach be expressed elsewhere in church life as well. It is possible to teach in ways that strive to present the doctrinal, moral and spiritual content of Christian faith with an openness to questioning and exploration. Sermons that include the possibility of discussion and a time for open questions may be more nerve-racking for those delivering them, but they may engage the people listening better, and may prove to be a more worthwhile learning experience for everyone. Ongoing discussion can also be done online with chat-rooms and Internet forums, as well as more face-to-face encounters in group settings.

This kind of combination of clear Christian convictions, with a confident and unashamed statement of core Christian belief, along with an openness to invite questions and questioners, to encourage personal stories, experiences and doubts to be aired and taken seriously, is a vital aspect of church life both theologically and strategically. It will be the fruit of listening carefully to the voices of those who stand outside the church, and the God who dwells within it.

Notes to Chapter 8

1. The great fourth-century theologian Athanasius makes a similar point in his *On the Incarnation*.
2. The word *dogma* is a Greek word that can simply mean a decree, decision or command. None of these words carries particularly negative connotations today, though 'dogma' is usually thought to be a bad thing!
3. Ellen Charry, *By the Renewing of Your Minds* (OUP, 1997).
4. Ibid., p. 105.
5. A classic example of these from the middle of the fourth century is the 'Catechetical Lectures' of Cyril of Jerusalem.
6. Andrew Louth (ed.), *Early Christian Writings*, Penguin Classics (Penguin, 1987), p. 191.
7. For a brief account of the catechumenate in the early church, see Stuart G. Hall, *Doctrine and Practice in the Early Church* (SPCK, 1991), pp. 15–22.
8. This theme is explored in a book by Graham Tomlin, shortly to be published by Continuum Books, entitled *Spiritual Fitness*.
9. Stanley Hauerwas, *After Christendom* (Abingdon Press, 1999), p. 98.
10. See, for example, the way Jesus tells the Parable of the Sower in Matthew 13:1–23.

CONCLUSION: CARRY ON DOUBLE-LISTENING

Double-listening is a tricky affair. On the one hand, paying too much attention to the world and not enough to the Word turns the church into a shallow, market-driven, God-lite organization, an agreeably unchallenging spiritual service provider whose lack of any real content demands that it follows fads and fashions for fear of seeming irrelevant. In the (surely vain) hope of gaining the world, it loses its soul.

On the other hand, listening to the Word whilst ignoring the world, not only runs the danger of turning the church into a self-serving, irrelevant and introspective institution whose incomprehensible rules of etiquette insulate its members from the outside world and alienate the outside world from its members, but also, paradoxically, stops Christians from actually *hearing* the Word. If, as this book has argued, Christianity is a resolutely material or incarnational faith, to listen to the Word actually demands listening to the world. To do otherwise is subtly to deny that the eternal Word became flesh and lived in the world.

In much the same way as paying serious attention to the Word will point us towards the world, the Bible is alert to the way in which listening to the world points us in the direction of the Word, albeit ambiguously and indecisively. 'The heavens declare the glory of God; the skies proclaim the work of his hand,' as the oft-quoted Psalm 19 puts it. Properly speaking, double-listening should be a symbiotic process, each part encouraging and learning from the other.

That does not, however, make it a straightforward process, nor one that terminates at the end of a book, let alone one as short as this. The two processes that stand behind this book – interviewing non-Christians (which includes people who call themselves Christian but don't know Christ in any meaningful sense of the word) and reading Scripture in order to respond to their opinions and doubts, as well as to provide the doctrinal, moral and spiritual resources to help us live well – are both ongoing.

The first was conducted in an official and formal manner, with professional recruiters, respondent incentives, trained interviewers, recording equipment and interview transcription all being used in the process. Such factors are essential for the manner in which the research was used in this book, but that should not discourage others from conducting their own, less formal interviews. These need not be with previously unknown respondents, or in a neutral setting, or even according to a set of prepared questions. Indeed, they may best be little more than semi-structured conversations.

One of the commonest responses, particularly among those interviewed in one-to-one sessions in the *Beyond the Fringe* project, was how pleased people were to have an opportunity to talk about such things. So busy were their lives that such topics usually lay buried under the weight of stress and routine, in spite of the fact that many recognized their importance.

The very act of initiating the process, making the practical arrangements and, above all, actually *listening* to people was welcomed. In itself, it was a powerful gesture that modelled a community that offers stillness, depth and an opportunity for people to explore their spiritual thoughts without fear of judgment. The motivation for such interviews must always be to listen to and perhaps connect with people where they are, rather than to show how sensitive or responsive the church is. But having noted that, it is worth observing how such a process can itself be an act of discipleship, imitating a God who is slow to judge and who, when he walked among us, asked penetrating questions and listened attentively to the answers.

To that end, Appendix 1 offers some ideas for those who might want to carry on 'world-listening' in their own situations. It contains practical advice as well as a list of questions that were used for the research behind this book. None of this is intended to be prescriptive but instead it offers ideas for those who wish to adopt and adapt them in their own contexts, or even just to ask their friends what they really think about God.

The second element within the book, listening to the Word, is one that needs constant attention. The Word of God is often described in Scripture as a light, and the point of light is not to look at it (you tend to get blinded if you do), but to look at other things in the light it sheds. So we are to look at our world, and what it thinks, in the light of what the Scriptures teach. Or to use another metaphor, Scripture can act like a pair of spectacles through which we are to view the world we live in – the point of spectacles is again, not to examine them for their own beauty of design, colour and handiwork, but to look at other things *through* them.

This means two kinds of reading. There is the reading of Scripture that simply tries to get to know it as well as possible. We read Scripture day after day, to become familiar with it, to fill our minds with it, to memorize it, so that it frequently comes to mind as we interact with people, books, art and opinions. In fact there is little chance of real growth in 'double listening' or indeed any kind of Christian maturity, without a regular habit of reading a section of the Bible just about every day. There is little likelihood of a major spiritual or apologetic engagement with our society without a much greater level of biblical literacy among ordinary Christians. If biblical literacy is fast vanishing in the wider culture, all the more reason for Christians to live and breathe Scripture's air, to soak it up, to know it by heart.

The second kind of reading works the other way. It involves going to the Bible with the questions raised by those we talk to. What is there in the Bible that speaks to the person who feels God is impersonal and cold? Does it offer resources for thinking as a Christian about loneliness, the fragmenting of society, the notion that science and religion are incompatible or that real Christians are aggressive and naïve? This is what reading the world through the eyes of the Scriptures can mean. Appendix 2 offers some passages from the

Bible, and some questions emerging out of the themes of the book to help begin that kind of attentive reading of the Bible.

It is hoped that the ideas within this book and the suggestions in the two appendices will help Christians in the process of double-listening and, in doing so, will help you in the task of building up a church that is responsive both to God and to the people he loves.

APPENDIX 1: LISTENING TO THE WORLD

For those readers interested in pursuing the idea of conducting research or simply listening to non- (or fringe-) Christians in their area, the following issues need to be considered.

Topic

What do you actually want to achieve? It is best to have a stated objective, preferably a narrow one, that shapes your approach. Do you want to explore people's attitude to *the* church, or *your* church, or to specific Christian beliefs? Do you want to assess people's innate spirituality and the part it plays in their lives? Do you want to adopt a more social angle, assessing their knowledge, understanding and opinion of the various services that the church (or your church) puts on in the local community? Or do you want to expand on this by exploring people's attitudes to social order and cohesion? (If those to whom we spoke were typical, interviewees will have a lot to say about the state of the nation and issues such as family stability, community cohesion, respect and discipline!) Whichever area you choose, try to articulate it – both what the topic is and what your objectives are – in a couple of short paragraphs.

The better you know your direction, the more likely you are to arrive there.

Teamwork

Don't do it alone. Try to sell the vision to friends and other members of your congregation. Get official support for it! A teamwork approach helps you to speak to more interviewees, compare and analyse what you learn, and share your findings and their implications with your church. Although the whole research process has benefits in simply educating church-goers about the issue in hand, it can have even greater benefit if it gives direction to a church's doctrinal, moral or spiritual focus.

Interviewees

Think about whom you wish to speak to. How are they defined? By their sex? By their age? By their lifestage (e.g. student, pre-family, early-family etc.)? By their occupation (student, full-time worker, part-time worker, unemployed, retired etc.)? By their beliefs (fringe Christian, uncommitted theist, spiritual person, disinterested agnostic etc.)? It is usually best to focus on one set of criteria and allow the others to fall out naturally, rather than attempting to cover all the bases, which can get very complex.

How many do you want to talk to? Robust studies require at least forty respondents, but unless you are planning to analyse and publish your research for wider consumption, this need not be a consideration. Try to go for *at least* a dozen people, spread evenly over the criteria of choice.

How do you get to speak to them? (This is the question that people invariably ask about qualitative research.) Ideally, interviewees are recruited by professional recruiters, but this is both unnecessarily expensive and too formal for the kind of 'world-listening' advocated here. Instead, a process known as 'snowballing' should be satisfactory. This is when a friend asks a friend (to ask a friend etc.) if they are 'within sample' and willing to give up the time for an interview. If the subject and objective of the project have been clearly articulated, as advised above, this gives the research a slightly (but much-needed) formal touch, convincing otherwise sceptical interviewees that it is not a surreptitious strategy for evangelism or worse.

Interviews

These can be as long as necessary, although it is best to keep them under an hour (anywhere between thirty minutes and one hour should be sufficient). That said, *Beyond the Fringe* interviews officially lasted an hour, but interviewees regularly stayed on for longer, chatting informally about the subjects in hand.

Try to conduct the interview in either a neutral place or, better still, on the interviewee's home territory.

As an interviewer you need to be sensitive to interviewees' background, level of knowledge and interest, and their inhibitions and nervousness. The questions must not be aggressive in any way, although if the interview proceeds well, interviewees often give implicit permission to ask searching questions (these cannot be asked at the start of an interview!).

Questions should be open ('How do you feel . . .?') rather than closed ('Do you think that . . .?'). Don't be afraid of silences. One of the objectives of such interviews is to offer a space for contemplation. You will soon become aware when a space for contemplation becomes an embarrassing silence!

Audio-record the interviews if you want to and if the interviewee has no objection. (If you do, you must emphasize that the recordings are for your ears only, and are destroyed as soon as the project is completed.) Alternatively (or ideally, in addition), take copious notes as you conduct the interview – they will help you remember what the interviewee said (or help you locate it on the tape) whilst sending the message that you are interested in what the interviewee has to say. Occasionally (rarely), an interviewee will object to this, in which case you will need to write a full report of the interview as soon as you can afterwards – memory will fade very quickly, particularly if you are doing more than a couple of interviews.

Questions

Beyond the Fringe, one of the two research projects used for this book, asked a range of questions, some of which are given below as an example of the kind of thing you might want to ask. Remember, just because you have a question, it doesn't mean you have to ask it. The objective of such one-to-one research is not to cover all the questions but to get the interviewee talking openly, honestly and fruitfully about the key issues.

What does your week look like? Where do you spend your week and whom do you mix with? What are the high points? What are the low or stressful points? What do you do to relax? What in the last month have you done that has given you a peaceful feeling? What in the last month has left you feeling frustrated?

What sorts of things matter to you? What makes you angry? Who and what do you admire? What do you think people should be like? What would you like your friends to say about you on your seventieth birthday?

As you look around at the world, what causes you concern? Who or what do you think is responsible for these things? What contribution do you think you could make to solving the problems you see? How do you see things developing in the future?

Why is it important to be good? Are there any things that are always right or wrong? What do you think happens after we die? How far do you feel the way you live will make an ultimate difference?

Some people think that everything happens by chance and others think that events happen according to some sort of plan. What do you think? Who or what is in charge? What guides your life? How do you make decisions about what to do? To what extent do you think things in this world are designed? What one big question do you wish there was an answer to?

What do you understand by the word 'God'? How can people relate to God? How would you say you do? Can you communicate with God? If so, what difference does it make? Have you ever had a sense of God and if so, where and when? If you had to talk to an alien about God and religious faith, how would you describe it?

Who do you believe Jesus to be? What difference has Jesus made to this world? What do you think the Bible is all about? Do you believe in heaven and, if so, what is it like?

What do you understand and feel about prayer, angels, meditation, ghosts, miracles, aliens etc.? What supernatural experiences have you or any close or trusted friends or relatives had? How do you explain these? What experiences or places have given you a sense of awe?

How do you feel when you go into a church or cathedral? What experience have you had of being in church? About 70% of people in this country believe in God but only 10% go to church. Why do you think this is? What's keeping them away? What should church be like? What is the role of church in society? Describe what a typical Christian is like and how you think they should be.

APPENDIX 2: LISTENING TO THE WORD

Section 1: God
Read Romans 8:5–17; 1 Corinthians 2:1–16; John 14:15–21.

- According to these passages, what are the Holy Spirit's main tasks or roles in the Christian life?
- What do these passages and their teaching on the Holy Spirit say to those searching for spiritual reality today?
- How would you answer someone who simply said he or she could not imagine what God is like?
- What changes might your church make to make it more receptive to those searching for spiritual reality today?

Section 2: Christianity
Read Acts 17:16–32; 1 Peter 3:13–16; Colossians 4:2–6.

- What do these passages tell us about how we are to go about answering the questions and objections of those who do not believe in Christ?

- Why do you think the early church was comparatively successful in getting its message across to a sceptical world?
- Can you think of examples of good Christian communication to a non-Christian audience? What makes it good or effective?
- What kind of help do you need to be able to answer effectively the questions you might be asked about your faith?

Section 3: Christians
Read Daniel 6:6–16; Romans 12:9–21; 1 Peter 2:9–21.

- Does the public image of Christianity really matter?
- How do these passages depict the living of public Christian life? What characteristics do they offer that might change the negative image of Christians today?
- In what ways might you practise your Christian faith more publicly?
- What would it take for people in your area to notice the presence of the church as a force for good in the local community?

Section 4: Church
Read Matthew 12:1–13; Luke 11:1–13; Acts 2:42–47.

- What do the first two stories tell us about *how* Jesus went about teaching people?
- How would people today react to a church like the one depicted in the passage from Acts? Is it realistic for the church today to aim to be like that?
- In what ways might your church embody some of the aspects of church in Acts 2?
- Chapter 8 mentions three kinds of teaching: *doctrinal, moral* and *spiritual.* Are all three necessary? Which do you think is most important? Which is missing from the church today, and why?

BIBLIOGRAPHY

Section 1: God

Astin, Howard. *Body and Cell: Making the Transition to Cell Church: A First Hand Account*. London: Monarch Books, 2002.

Coupland, Douglas. *Generation X: Tales for an Accelerated Culture*. London: Abacus, 1992.

Frost, Rob. *Essence*. London: Kingsway, 2002.

Green, Michael (ed.). *Church without Walls: A Global Examination of Cell Church*. Carlisle: Paternoster, 2002.

Hornby, Nick. *How to Be Good*. London: Penguin, 2001.

Potter, Phil. *The Challenge of Cell Church: Getting to Grips with Cell Church Values*. Oxford: Bible Reading Fellowship, 2001.

Ward, Pete. *Liquid Church*. Carlisle: Paternoster, 2002.

Section 2: Christianity

Grant, Robert M. *Greek Apologists of the Second Century*. Philadelphia: Westminster, 1988.

McGrath, Alister E. *Dawkins' God*. Oxford: Blackwell, 2004.

—. *The Twilight of Atheism: The Rise and Fall of Disbelief in the Modern World*. New York: Doubleday, 2004.

Stackhouse, John. *Humble Apologetics: Defending the Faith Today*. Oxford: OUP,
    2002.
Tomlin, Graham. *The Provocative Church*. London: SPCK, 2002.

Section 3: Christians
Newbigin, Lesslie. *The Gospel in a Pluralist Society*. London: SPCK, 1989.
Stevenson, J. (ed.). *A New Eusebius: Documents Illustrative of the History of the
    Church to AD 337*. London: SPCK, 1957.

Section 4: Church
Charry, Ellen. *By the Renewing of Your Minds*. New York: OUP, 1997.
Cyril of Jerusalem. 'The catechetical lectures of St Cyril', in *Nicene and Post-
    Nicene Fathers*. Oxford: Parker, 1894.
Hall, Stuart G. *Doctrine and Practice in the Early Church*. London: SPCK, 1991.
Louth, Andrew (ed.). *Early Christian Writings*, Penguin Classics.
    Harmondsworth: Penguin, 1987.